THE SWEDISH ROOM

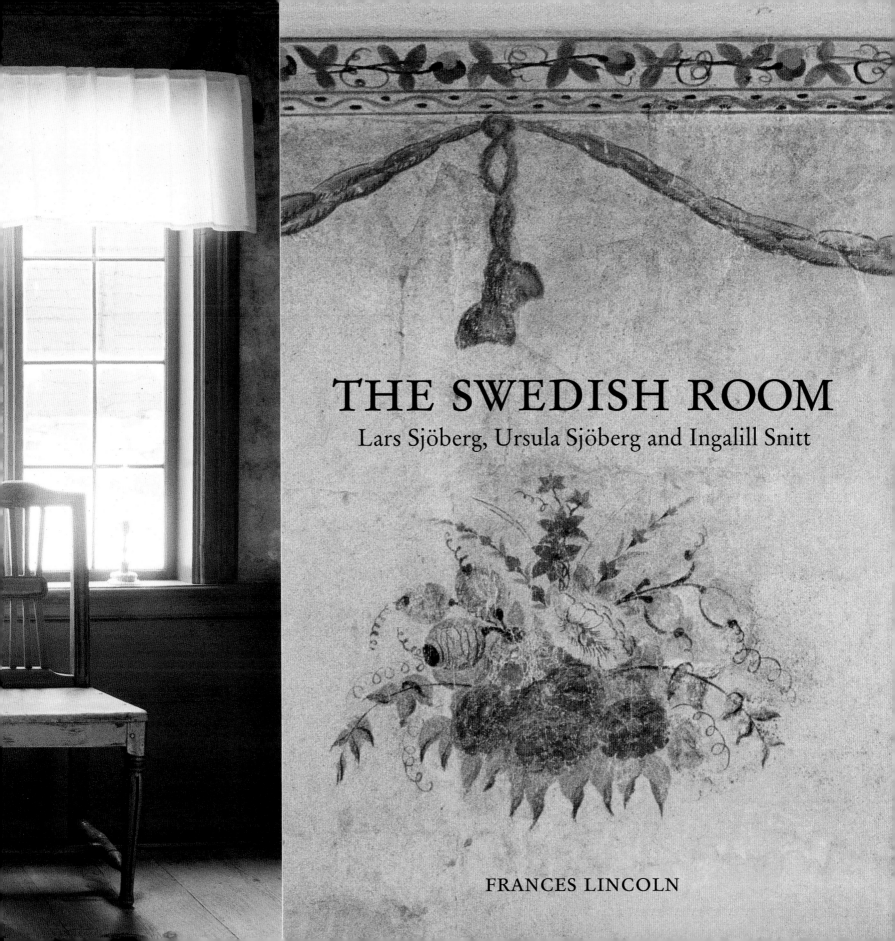

THE SWEDISH ROOM

Lars Sjöberg, Ursula Sjöberg and Ingalill Snitt

FRANCES LINCOLN

Frances Lincoln Limited 1994
4 Torriano Mews, Torriano Avenue, London NW5 2RZ

Translated from the original Swedish manuscript by Ian Hinchliffe

British Library cataloguing-in-publication data
A catalogue record for this book is available from the British Library.

ISBN 0-7112-0915-4

Set in Stempel Garamond by Frances Lincoln Limited
Printed in Hong Kong
First published by Frances Lincoln Limited: September 1994
5 7 9 8 6 4

PAGE 1 *False stoves – usually painted wood cupboards made to look like mirror-images of real stoves – were commonly used in the eighteenth century to achieve symmetry. This one is from Odenslunda (see page 186).*

PAGES 2–3 *The bedroom in a cottage in Hälsingland was decorated in the 1830s by one of the many skilled itinerant rural painters who continued to use delicate Gustavian decorative schemes decades after they had first appeared in the capital.*

THIS PAGE AND OPPOSITE *The simplicity of the pure white stucco ceiling at Hässelbyholm is typical of the 1670s.*

CONTENTS

As part of the recent renovations at Ekensberg manor on the shores of Lake Mälaren, layers of wallpaper were removed in one of the anterooms to reveal the original late-eighteenth-century decoration. The subtle charm of the painting is typical of the somewhat restrained but perfectly judged interiors of the late Gustavian era. The walls above a wooden dado are covered in coarse linen panels that provided a good smooth surface for painting. The portrait represents Gustav III and the plaster bust his brother Duke Carl (later Carl XIII). The grey-painted chairs were made in Stockholm in the 1790s and are signed by the chair maker, Johan Hammarström.

INTRODUCTION

The task of presenting a picture of Swedish interior decoration from a historical perspective is challenging, but stimulating. It is one that could not have been undertaken without close collaboration with the photographer, and in many cases the photographic content inspired the text.

Our aim has been to show the rich legacy of domestic settings that have been preserved in the castles, stately homes, manors, farmhouses and summer retreats of Sweden. Some of the rooms illustrated have retained their original furnishings intact, others are the result of careful reconstructions or reproductions. While it is, of course, the authentic *milieux* which possess the greatest intrinsic value, reconstructions such as those in the Skansen open-air museum in Stockholm are sometimes better able to do justice to domestic lifestyles which have otherwise been irretrievably lost. This is especially true of Swedish rural culture.

Some familiarity with how the Swedish home was planned and run is essential in order to understand the different characteristics of the rooms. Regardless of their size, Swedish houses can, by and large, trace their pedigrees back either to the *parstuga*, dating from the sixteenth century, or to the six-room ground plans of larger, late seventeenth-century homes. The *parstuga*, or 'double cottage', consisted of two adjacent but distinct sections, linked and separated by an entrance hall, which divided the everyday living quarters from the 'best rooms'. The six-room ground plan, which provided the basis for many of the manor houses, placed the 'best room' or *salle* in the centre of the building. The *salle*, which was primarily reserved for banquets, linked separate suites for the lord and lady of the house. The most extravagant decoration was found in the lady's apartments, and particularly in what was essentially her drawing room. By the end of the eighteenth century, French influence prevailed and this drawing room had evolved into a larger, general reception room, the *salon.*

One of the book's ambitions is to show how decorating ideals in Sweden have been characterized by a resolve to translate European taste into a more austere Swedish vocabulary. Sweden's Age of Greatness in the seventeenth century may have given the country's architecture and interior design a fillip, but it was not until Sweden was once again plunged into poverty during the following century that a more consummate aesthetic made its mark, stimulated by the need – and desire – to make the country become self-reliant. It was a time when foreign influences were uncompromisingly adapted to Swedish conditions: pine floors were installed in place of oak parquet; furniture was modelled on imported pieces, but developed along more utilitarian lines which could be copied by less accomplished provincial craftsmen; and, on the walls, carved wooden panelling and precious silks were replaced by painted canvases. These panels became the hallmark of eighteenth-century Swedish interiors. The skilful decorative artists, trained by French masters initially recruited to assist with the decoration of the Royal Palace in Stockholm, were much in demand throughout the country. In time, the work they did provided the foundation for a new, Swedish tradition of painted decor.

The paints used for ceilings and walls were either oil paints based chiefly on linseed oil, or a kind of distemper made from a mixture of powdered chalk, glue and pigments. During the course of the eighteenth century, the rich, full-bodied palette of Baroque colours gave way, first to a predominance of light yellow, and later to light grey.

Exquisitely decorated rooms in royal palaces and stately homes of the Gustavian era set the tone for more modest settings. With chalk-based paints and a sheaf of brushes, a painter in the 1780s could bestow lasting elegance on the humblest of interiors. Sörby Manor in Närke comprises only three rooms and a kitchen, yet it can still boast laurel wreaths in the salon, garlands of flowers in the anteroom and curling vines in the bedroom. It is a testament to the way in which the decorating fashions of the court and the capital city spread into the provinces and permeated every layer of society.

Regal splendour has always attracted attention and applause, and though a number of sumptuous settings are described and illustrated here, we have made a conscious effort to lay the emphasis on more modest interiors. What is most striking is the chaste majesty of their decoration – a grandeur which does not rely on size for its effect, and the evidence that they provide of the ascetic simplicity of everyday life. It is, perhaps, precisely these qualities that are quintessentially Swedish.

1640 – 1720

THE STIRRINGS OF

The impact of Italian Baroque and French Absolutism

INTERNATIONAL STYLE

At the conclusion of the Thirty Years' War in 1648, Sweden emerged as one of the key players in Europe's political arena, its newly acquired territories around the Baltic Sea bringing it into direct contact with the contemporary cultural trends of Northern Europe. Together with success in war came an increasing prosperity, and the following half-century, now referred to in Sweden as the Age of Greatness, brought with it the consolidation of royal power as well as the emergence of a style of architecture and interior decoration that was for the first time distinctively Swedish.

As the war drew to a close, there was an enormous expansion in the building of homes. Stockholm was rapidly outgrowing its medieval city walls and the government awarded spectacular plots of land along the shores of the old island city to beneficiaries who were expected to raise palatial new stone buildings to give to what was, at the time, a rather dreary and antiquated city, a skyline which better befitted the ambitions of a burgeoning military power.

Initially there were no Swedish architectural prototypes to follow. So the Swedes turned for inspiration to those European nations affected by the Renaissance. This is why, when he returned home from the wars, General Wrangel modelled his castle of Skokloster on Ujazdow Palace, the summer residence of the Polish royal family, built outside Warsaw in 1624. The rooms decorated for Wrangel boast gilded leather or rich woven tapestry wallcoverings, stone floors and heavily sculpted colourful stucco ceilings. Most splendid of all are the carved and painted chimneypieces, the designs for which were taken either from Dutch, German or Italian engravings of the early 1630s. Indeed, although the rooms at Skokloster, like most buildings constructed in Sweden between 1630 and 1660, attempted to appear as modern as any in Europe, they actually embodied the styles that had been current in Northern Europe half a century earlier. New ideas in decorating seeped northwards only slowly. The desire to be in step with Europe may have contributed to the fact that it was not until the mid-1650s that a recognizably Swedish style began to make itself felt. This found its greatest exponents in the architects Tessin the Elder and Tessin the Younger, who were to dominate Swedish architecture and interior decoration throughout the second half of the century.

Father and son together evolved a style that was clearly influenced by the Classically inspired Baroque architecture that they saw on their many trips to Italy and France. Typical exteriors designed by them had rendered walls enlivened by rustication (that is, made to look like blocks of masonry divided by deep joints), Classically derived window settings (incorporating, for example, Ionic or Doric details) and a uniquely Swedish version of the Mansard roof, the *säteri* roof. In this form of roof, the gentle slope is interrupted by a narrow vertical wall pierced by small windows, making a double slope (see page 31).

PREVIOUS PAGES *The ceiling decoration at Sjöö Manor includes the initials of Johan Gabriel Stenbock, who commissioned the work in the 1670s. The bas-relief effect is achieved by painting on cloth and wood.*
LEFT AND ABOVE *Much of the decoration at Skokloster was backward-looking and, by comparison with the innovations at Sjöö, for example, must have seemed somewhat passé even at the time it was done in the 1660s. The stucco detail in the* salle *(ABOVE) and the painted walls and ceilings of the top-floor rooms are more Renaissance than Baroque in style. Similar ceilings could be seen in many far more modest houses between 1630 and 1650. A number of rooms on the top floor were redecorated in the 1830s using the original scheme as a guide.*

LEFT *The walls of this anteroom at Skokloster, which has retained its original colours, were hung with gilded leather in the mid-seventeenth century. The six-panelled door and the wall panels with their symmetrical gold-coloured floral arrangements on a dark background are a reflection of the era's concern to emulate fashionable French interpretations of Classical Roman ideals. In more sumptuous settings, the door panels might well have been carved and gilded. The floor is paved with limestone quarried on the Swedish island of Öland.*

OPPOSITE *This detail comes from a chimneypiece of 1657-8 from the castle at Skokloster. Sculpted in wood and then painted to mimic marble, it is a monumental construction in the Renaissance tradition, flanked by columns terminating in children's faces and voluted cartouches. The detail showing the monogram of Countess Anna Maria von Haugwitz was added about fifteen years later. Most of the chimneypieces of the latter half of the seventeenth century used sandstone from the Swedish island of Gotland, similarly carved and then painted in oils.*

Despite Tessin the Elder's most important commissions being the palaces of Drottningholm and Strömsholm, both built in the 1660s, perhaps more significant for Sweden's architectural heritage was his creation, during the course of the 1670s, of a new type of country house in the style of Palladio's interpretation of a Roman country villa. This found its ideal in Sjöö Manor in Uppland, north-west of Stockholm, which was begun in 1673. Tessin deliberately chose a sloping site so that the front of the building had an impressive three storey façade, while the other side had just two storeys, allowing the *salle* to lead straight into the garden. Sjöö Manor was truly the first country house that was neither fort nor farm but acknowledged a new, affluent, leisurely way of life.

During the last quarter of the seventeenth century the influence of the Tessins also came to dominate interior design. Their work was characterized by proportions in the ratios of 2:3 or 3:5, held to be ideal in the Classical world. Ceilings were often of white stucco with cornices of painted and sculpted wood or plaster, or of canvas painted to emulate bas-relief carvings. Fireplaces and chimneypieces were either carved in sandstone or painted to resemble stone, and were embellished with Classically inspired motifs such as stylized leaves arranged in patterns. Even doors, doorframes and panels were decorated with similar motifs in *grisaille* or with cameos on coloured backgrounds. The walls of the most important rooms were covered with embossed and gilded leather, or with high-warp tapestries featuring figures or woodland scenes. Gilded leather began to make its mark in Sweden towards the middle of the seventeenth century and retained its popularity well into the 1750s. Large expanses of wall in less important rooms might be covered in wool fabric woven in repeated patterns, while those of staircases, entrance halls and salons were often painted – on linen or directly on the plaster or timber – to imitate either woven wallcoverings or to simulate marble embellished with elements such as *faux* pilasters, piers and niches.

Stucco became one of the mainstays of Swedish architecture at that time. One of the era's most skilful practitioners in this material was the Italian-born Carlo Carove who worked on the main staircase at Drottningholm. Carove and his fellow artists used *putti*, laurel swags, Corinthian pilasters and other elements borrowed from Classical architecture, to create a magnificence unequalled elsewhere.

The floors of important houses at this time were most often made of oak or pine boards laid diagonally, although main bedrooms or small studies (often called cabinets) were sometimes laid with parquetry. Entrance halls and the larger banqueting rooms might have floors of stone or imported marble laid in geometric patterns.

As the design of the buildings looked to Europe for inspiration, so did the loose furnishings. Until about 1680, chairs followed the Dutch example and were leather-covered with rectangular upholstered backs. After this, however, Dutch-English influenced lacquered chairs with cane panels or rush seats began to increase in popularity, and by 1700 were as common as the traditional upholstered models. Cabinets often came from Northern Germany and the Lowlands and were made of oak, walnut or pine, painted and veined to resemble the grain of hardwoods. In the bedroom the French ideal reigned supreme: enclosed by fabric, possibly *en suite* with the wallhangings, beds were the focus of the room and often formed an integral part of it, usually set in an alcove.

The influence of the Tessins' work gradually spread, and can be discerned in many of the far more modest manor

houses built during the late seventeenth and early eighteenth centuries. These smaller houses were generally single-storey timber buildings painted with a distinctive dark red iron-oxide paint known as 'Falu' red, after the central Swedish town where it was first produced. They were distinguished by the same high sloping *säteri* roofs as their grander neighbours, and with ground plans that echo the symmetry of the Tessins' layout, but on a smaller scale. There were usually five main rooms, the largest of which would be the centrally placed *salle*. In many cases this *salle* would lie behind the entrance hall and project towards the garden, imitating the

appearance of Sjöö. The kitchen, meanwhile, was kept in a smaller, separate building to minimize the risk of fire.

Between 1680 and 1682 an almost fatal blow was dealt to the construction of stately homes. To compensate for the country's failing economy, the state began to recall the grants of land it had been assigning to the nobility since the Middle Ages. Once confiscated, this land was lent to officers of state in lieu of salary. This effectively called a halt to almost all major new building projects for the next forty years. Two of the very few exceptions, Steninge and Sturefors, both herald a new direction in interior decorating.

OPPOSITE *Although not installed until 1663-4, the high-relief stucco ceiling in the* salle *at Skokloster is almost Renaissance in character. Around a centrepiece depicting the biblical story of Daniel slaying a monster are four roundels, each with a vignette of one of the four continents then known. Two of these, Africa symbolized by a crocodile and America by an armadillo, can be seen here. The chandelier hanging from the jaws of the dragon was made in Stockholm some time during the 1670s at the glassworks of Melchior Ljung.*

ABOVE RIGHT *The wooden cornice and a section of the ceiling's painted* faux *moulding at Sjöö was produced some ten years after the stucco ceiling in the* salle *at Skokloster and illustrates the move towards more Classical taste. The bas-relief effect is repeated on the doors, panels and other features in the room.*

ABOVE LEFT *The cherubic heads crowned with baskets of fruit on a ceiling at Nynäs Manor in Södermanland testify that the art of the stuccoists was not confined to producing architectural friezes during the 1670s. All the ceilings at Nynäs are whitewashed, a development away from the polychromatic schemes of the earlier years of the century.*

Sandemar

ABOVE *Sandemar is a miniature version of the palatial stone mansions of the Baroque era. The allegorical wooden sculptures in the formal gardens are all painted white to suggest marble.*

LEFT *The walls of the entrance hall are painted with* trompe l'oeil *pilasters and shadowy landscapes while the ceilings under the stairs are painted in grisaille to imitate the bas-relief of Classical friezes. The two painted figures, cut out of wood, once served as garden ornaments.*

Sandemar Manor, near Dalarö in the southern
reaches of the Stockholm skerries, was
commissioned by Gabriel Falkenberg towards the
end of the seventeenth century, and its
exceptionally well-preserved interiors are a
testament to the strength of the prevailing Baroque
taste. Its appearance is deceptive, for beneath the
later addition of a lath and plaster cladding that
gives it the air of a stone house, Sandemar is a
timbered building. Initially, the horizontally laid
timbers would have been exposed and painted red.

The front façade of the main building looks
down on the *cour d'honneur* which is framed on
two other sides by pairs of single-storey detached
wings and square pavilions. The other side of the
house looks out over one of the best-maintained
private Baroque gardens in Sweden. The formal
layout of the garden and even the allegorical
wooden sculptures are still much as they appear in
an engraving of *c.*1700. The importance of the
house in relation to its surroundings is accentuated
by the avenues lined with trees and the paths
between clipped shrubs that radiate out from – and
lead back to – the house.

The symmetry of the garden is echoed in the
layout of the interior, especially in the double
staircase of the entrance hall. The lower *salle* lies in
the centre of the house on the ground floor, where
it enjoys views over the garden to the Baltic Sea
beyond, and the upper *salle* is immediately above
it. There are prime examples of the three principle
types of Baroque wall decoration at Sandemar:
paint applied directly onto boards in *grisaille* in the
entrance hall; *faux* Gobelin tapestries painted on
stretched linen in the upper *salle*, and gilded
embossed leather in the dining room. In no other
private house is the spectrum of the taste of this
period so clearly seen.

LEFT *The walls of the upper* salle *at Sandemar are covered with coarse linen cloth stretched over a frame and painted to resemble high-warp tapestry, a form of imitation which was especially common towards the end of the seventeenth century. The motifs chosen in this instance are from the Old Testament story of Solomon. At Sandemar, as elsewhere, oil paintings were used to fill out the space above the low, wide doors. Single doors like these, with four vertical panels, remained in vogue until the middle of the eighteenth century. The blue-and-white decorative fillet round the doors echoes the painted ornamentation of the canvas ceiling, wooden cornice and skirting boards.*

OVERLEAF *New doors and new, higher dadoes were installed in the lower* salle *at Sandemar during the Gustavian period, and the plain white plaster ceiling replaces what was once a stretched linen cloth, painted in a fashion similar to those that line the walls of the upper* salle. *The sandstone chimneypiece has remained intact since the Baroque period, as has its fire-screen with its grisaille leaves against a red background. No doubt the chimneypiece and ceiling were once decorated in the same way as the screen.*

The high-backed chairs and gilded leather wallcoverings may well have been part of the original interior decoration. A detail of the gilded leather shows the complexity of its swirling design. The embossed leather was given a gold-coloured base, and other colours were applied on top of this.

NEW ALIGNMENTS

1720 – 1750

*Late Baroque and the influence
of England and the Orient*

After more than twenty years of a devastating war with Russia, Sweden signed a peace treaty in Nystad (now Uusikaupunki in Finland) in 1721. This ushered in a period of some fifty years, now known as the Age of Freedom, in which the government strove to maintain peace, and to foster national political and economic development. For a country ravaged by the effects of war, it was vital that trade in general, and the export of iron and timber in particular, should be stimulated. It was also a time when the powers of the King were so severely curtailed that he became a mere figurehead, leaving Arvid Bernhard Horn, the head of the government, as effective ruler.

Against this background, the style of the absolutist Bourbon court in France, which continued to lead the field in interior decoration, seemed appropriate only for the royal court and its immediate circle. The influence of Sweden's trading partners made itself more strongly felt. Sweden moved closer to England not only commercially through trade, but also ideologically – for Horn was a great admirer of English democracy. As far as interiors were concerned, mahogany furniture and woven cane chairs were the chief English imports. Gothenburg, the nation's premier port and second largest city, drew full advantage from its location on the Swedish west coast. Its relative ease of access to and trade with Western Europe and England left their mark on local architecture and craftsmanship and the city presented a far more English countenance – with many more unrendered brick houses – than the Francophile Stockholm.

The founding, in Gothenburg, of the Swedish East India Company in 1731 greatly stimulated interest in all things Chinese. With its armada of Swedish-built ships the Company found that not only could it satisfy domestic demand for porcelain, silks, tea and a whole host of herbs and spices, but it could also trade the surplus on the European market. European taste for *chinoiserie* had been developing since the end of the seventeenth century and now extended to furniture and whole interior schemes. Cargoes of lacquered cabinets, chests and tables made the long sea voyage to Sweden. Horn, who was a wealthy landowner with more than a passing interest in architecture, had the plastered walls of one of his rooms in Ekebyholm Castle, in Uppland, to the east of Stockholm, painted with Chinese-style panoramas in the 1730s. Chinese-inspired murals, by two German journeymen-artists, also appeared at Thureholm Manor on the Baltic coast, in the mid-1730s; and by 1753 Drottningholm, the royal family's summer palace, boasted a garden pavilion built and decorated exclusively in the Chinese idiom.

These burgeoning interests, discernible at first only in the houses of those wealthy enough to purchase imported furniture and utensils, brought new strands of richness to interior design. However, the decorating traditions that the Tessins had established continued to hold considerable sway until as

PREVIOUS PAGES *The painted shelf and the four plaster casts, which were originally fitted to the wall and used as consoles, were designed to display china in the porcelain kitchen at Thureholm in the 1740s (see page 34).*
LEFT *All the lavish decoration – including the 'tiles' that frame the swirling* rocaille *decorative patterns – in the bedchamber of Ekebyholm was painted directly on the walls in the 1740s. The stove, which was manufactured in the 1790s, was probably not installed until the late 1800s to replace the original fireplace.*
ABOVE *Real tiles, part of a consignment specially imported from Holland, were used to cover the walls from floor to ceiling in the salon at Bergshammar in the 1730s.*

late as the middle of the eighteenth century, even though Tessin the Younger died in 1728. Indeed, although it was built in the early 1700s and so strictly speaking predates the Age of Freedom, Sturefors in Östergötland, south-west of Stockholm, designed by Tessin the Younger, had inestimable influence on the concept of the ideal home as it developed over the first fifty years of the century. The Francophile Tessin had kept in close touch with developments in France and Sturefors boasted a magnificent painted ceiling in the new style of Jean Berain. Berain was a draughtsman-designer at the court of Louis XIV who brought a new vocabulary of ornament to interiors, seen in the curves and scrolls of lacy patterns that might include vases, feathers or stylized masks. Motifs like this were soon imitated and can be found on the painted wooden plank ceilings at Beatelund Manor on Ingarö Island in the Stockholm skerries and at Högbo Foundry in Gästrikland, north-west of Stockholm.

Tessin's design for the doors was also new: it called for the leaf to be divided into three panels, with smaller ones above and below a larger one in the middle, setting a style which was to endure throughout the first half of the eighteenth

century and can be seen, for example, in the porcelain kitchen at Thureholm. The wall decorations at Sturefors were also to have a far-reaching and long-lasting influence. Genuine Gobelin tapestries hung in the two anterooms on either side of the great *salle*. The bedchambers beyond were sumptuously decorated with silk brocatelle wallhangings in alternate fields of red and gold. Other rooms were originally hung with textiles: some of these took the form of painted imitations of Gobelin tapestries depicting hunting scenes, utopian woodlands, or cavalcades of historical and mythological figures. Elsewhere richly ornamented velvet wallhangings were used.

This variety of wallcovering at Sturefors was imitated in many ways depending on the affluence of the owner and the availability of local artists. Imaginative copies of Gobelin tapestries could be painted either on coarse linen or directly onto wooden walls. Flock wallcoverings, simulating patterned velvet, also became a common feature of contemporary homes. These consisted of lengths of linen fabric decorated with printed or stencilled patterns which were then coated with a glutinous substance over which finely shredded wool, or 'flock', was strewn in one or more colours.

Most of the smaller manor houses built after the peace treaty of 1721 were designed with six principal rooms – a central salon, to which access was gained via an entrance hall or vestibule, and two pairs of anterooms on either side. Kitchens continued to be housed in a separate building to reduce the very real risk of fire. Timber, used for floors, walls and ceilings, was by far the most common building material and long, hard winters dictated the need for open fires or stoves in every room. The wood exteriors also continued to be painted Falu red with only the grey or grey-white of the door and window frames offering any contrast.

Larger houses were usually built on similar lines, with an enfilade of the main rooms looking out towards the garden, but they might also have additional, separate, wings or annexes. During the latter half of the century some single-storey wooden houses were clad in vertical planks of wood painted yellow to feign the appearance of rendered stone

ABOVE *An urn spilling with spring flowers is one of the rare examples of a season represented on a painted ceiling of the 1740s at Ekebyholm. The masterly skill and newness of style evident in the work make it likely that it was done by one of the artists who had recently been employed on the redecoration of the Royal Palace in Stockholm, where the newest decorative style had been introduced from France during the 1730s.*

buildings. Others were aggrandized by an upper floor.

The manor house at Bergshammar in Södermanland is a good example of the many and varied cultural influences that pervaded Sweden at that time: the clerk of works, Joseph-Gabriel Destain, was French but would almost certainly have referred to drawings by both Tessin the Younger and Carl Hårleman, Tessin's successor as Court Architect. The walls in the *salle* are covered from dado to cornice with small Dutch tiles whose blue-and-white colouring was inspired by Chinese faience. Bergshammar also boasts wallpaper which was designed to imitate the effect of ceramic tiles, manufactured in Stockholm *c.* 1730.

By the middle of the 1730s, members of the Swedish gentry were importing such substantial quantities of wallcoverings, fabrics, furniture and ornaments to decorate their homes that, in 1739, the state set up a Manufacturing Office. This was to support and administer Swedish production of similar articles in an attempt to counter the economic effects of these expensive imports. In 1745 Jean Eric Rehn, a pioneer in fields as diverse as industrial espionage (for weaving looms and machinery), the design of faience, silver, textiles, furniture and even entire houses, was appointed its Artistic Director. His chief task was to handle commissions from the royal palaces and to produce pattern designs and technical solutions for the dozen or so Swedish silk mills, and for the Rörstrand faience factory in Stockholm. This had been set up in the 1720s, and, for the most part, turned out blue-and-white Chinese-inspired ornaments and tableware, as well as the North German type of tiled stoves.

Meanwhile, after a twenty-year hiatus, work had started again in 1728 on the half-finished Royal Palace in Stockholm and, in the late 1740s, on major building and decorating schemes at Drottningholm. The work of completing the palace was entrusted to Hårleman, who brought in artists and craftsmen from Paris so the decoration would be as up-to-the-minute as possible. However, apart from a few exceptions, the high Rococo style that these men brought with them was not to have much of an impact outside the royal household until well into the second half of the century.

BELOW *The* salle *or dining room at Thureholm, built in the 1730s, is one of Sweden's oldest early Rococo interiors still in private ownership. The imitation oak wainscoting is rounded in the corners of the room and is decorated with painted bronze-coloured trophies, and with crowns and laurel branches in the panels above the royal portraits. The overdoor carries a portrait of Queen Ulrika Eleonora the Elder, consort to King Carl XI, who is shown in the adjacent full-length portrait. To the right of him hangs a portrait of Carl XII in military uniform. All of these paintings were copied from older originals some time during the 1730s by Pasch the Elder, artist to the royal court.*

RIGHT *This detail is part of a mural painted directly onto the smooth plaster wall in a ground-floor room at Ekebyholm. It was commissioned by Arvid Bernhard Horn, then head of the Swedish government, who redecorated the house in the 1730s. Inspired by the Forbidden City in Peking, which gripped the European imagination during the first half of the eighteenth century, it also portrays unmistakably European parterres in the garden.*

Thureholm

ABOVE *A broad ramp leads over the stables to the courtyard enclosed by the three-storey main building and its two single-storey detached wings. The front façade bears all the hallmarks of the Swedish Rococo style: pediment-crowned, it is rendered and painted yellow with white embrasures round the windows, and is decorated with white pilaster strips. Originally all the windows had small panes of glass in putty casements like those retained in the wings. All the buildings have high, distinctive double-pitch säteri roofs, the upper parts clad in sheet metal, the lower in brick tiles.*

LEFT *The billiard room is decorated with grandiose Chinese landscapes and city scenes divided by elaborately painted frames surrounded by red and black imitations of oriental lacquerwork. The wallpaintings are the work of Johann Klein, a master craftsman who specialized in this type of motif using sources from his native Germany as well as from France and Italy. The overdoors used to be hung with portraits of the Bielke family, but have been replaced in our own century by paintings inspired by the original decor.*

Thureholm sits high above a terraced rock slope on the shores of the Baltic near to Trosa in Södermanland. Built on the site of an older house that was burnt in 1719 by marauding Russian troops, it was one of the first major private building projects to be completed after the peace treaty of 1721, and was to prove one of the most expensive in Sweden at that time. The Bielke family had owned Thureholm since the 1500s, and Thure Gabriel Bielke commissioned Hårleman to design and supervise the rebuilding work in 1728. Work on the interiors took place throughout the 1730s and into the 1740s – the period that saw the transition between the style of the late Baroque and that of the early Rococo, when the vogue for *chinoiserie* was beginning to sweep through Europe. Although most of the household effects were sold off around the time of the First World War, Thureholm remains an unusually eloquent example of an early eighteenth-century Swedish home.

A pilastered vestibule runs the full length of the main building on the garden side, opening out onto the south-facing terrace.

The rooms on the middle floor were the principal living quarters, grouped around the wood-panelled *salle*. The most extravagantly decorated rooms are the anterooms and the state bedroom, the walls of which were covered with tapestries including some from Beauvais that were woven after originals by Jean Berain.

Painted linen wall decorations in the main bedroom were imported from Dresden during the 1730s. Landscapes enclosed by trompe l'oeil *gilt frames and cartouches* (FAR RIGHT) *are interspersed between the (unseen) main panels which illustrate the sacking of Troy.* (NEAR RIGHT) *Between marble columns furnished with consoles bearing urns and busts, Apollo stands with his lyre against a background of acanthus scrolls.*

The ground-floor porcelain kitchen at Thureholm was used both as a kitchen and as a cabinet for the family's precious collection of blue-and-white porcelain, specially imported from China. (Some of these pieces can now be seen at the Skansen open-air museum in Stockholm.) Decorated in the 1740s, it ranks as one of the most remarkable eighteenth-century rooms in Sweden. Not only are the walls covered from floor to ceiling in a willow-pattern of scenes inspired by tales from the Orient – flying dragons, mandarins and Chinese landscapes can be seen even behind the once-crowded plate shelves – but also the sideboards, doors and even such details as the brass candle sconces are painted in the same ubiquitous shades of blue and white.

The detail of a wall in the porcelain kitchen shows a boy in Chinese dress beside an imaginary tree painted above a plaster console. The recess just above the console was designed to hold a cup.

Olivehult

ABOVE *Nestling between avenues of tall lime trees, the front façade of Olivehult is dominated by its tiled Mansard roof. Some time early this century, small-paned casement windows were installed and the row of windows above the entrance door was added. At the same time the horizontal timbers of the façade were clad with vertical panels which have now been repainted red to restore the house to its original colour.*

LEFT *Although the extra storey was not added until the second half of the eighteenth century, the walls in the new upper* salle *were decorated with hangings from the early part of the century, giving the room a distinctly Baroque character. These oil-on-canvas painted imitations of high-warp tapestries were highly prized throughout the 1700s, a fact which perhaps explains why they were used even in a 'modern' setting. The scenes depicted here draw their inspiration from the Old Testament story of Esther and Ahasuerus. The gilded leather wallcoverings glimpsed in the bedroom beyond are also early eighteenth-century. Most of the furniture dates from the nineteenth century, but the chairs in the bedroom are pure Rococo.*

The manor house at Olivehult in Östergötland, south-west of Stockholm, is now a two-storey timber building: the ground floor was built in the seventeenth century, and the upper floor was added during the Gustavian era, probably in the 1780s. Some of the ground-floor rooms, especially the porcelain cabinet, lend a special significance to this house, since much of the decoration is late Baroque in flavour.

LEFT *The early-eighteenth century flock wallcovering in the lower* salle *consists of lengths of linen fabric stencilled in Berainesque patterns and strewn with finely shredded wool or 'flock'. This type of wallcovering, the unpolished deal floor and the whitewashed ceiling are features typical of smaller manor houses during the first half of the eighteenth century. The generously proportioned sideboard has doors at the front and on the sides and was probably made some time around 1800. Above it hangs a portrait of Bishop Jonas Linnerius, forefather of the Linnerhielm family who occupied the house in its heyday during the first half of the nineteenth century.*

RIGHT *The porcelain cabinet or plate room is Olivehult's greatest pearl: it still contains collections of tableware that live on only in the inventory lists of other manor houses. Until the end of the eighteenth century, any house's best tableware would invariably be made of pewter. Subsequently, English-produced creamware or Queen's ware became so popular that it gradually drove most of the pewterers and faience factories out of business, and the Swedish factory at Rörstrand was forced to produce large quantities of creamware in order to compete. Collected by the Linnerhielm family, these plates are the work of Swedish pewterers of the eighteenth and nineteenth centuries; the self-coloured tureens come from both the Rörstrand factory and from Leeds in England.*

1750 - 1770
PROGRESSIVE

The spread of French Rococo and the appeal of the exotic

REFINEMENTS

By the middle of the eighteenth century it was no longer unusual for new houses to be commissioned by clients outside the closed circle of the aristocracy. The successful export of Swedish products such as iron, timber and copper to a hungry world market had created a new class of prosperous citizens – the merchants and the mine-owners – who, by the 1750s, were able to convert their profits into bricks and mortar, and wished to show off their wealth and new-found status by building and decorating their houses in the latest fashion.

By this time the Rococo style that had begun in France in the early years of the century as an aristocratic expression of luxury had been introduced to Sweden by Carl Hårleman, through his work for the royal palaces during the 1730s and 1740s. In his hands the style took on a noticeably Swedish guise, and he emerged as its leading exponent. Through engravings of his designs and through the dispersal of the carvers, carpenters and painters who had worked closely with colleagues brought over from France by Hårleman to work on the Royal Palace in Stockholm, the Rococo rippled through the country, becoming modified as it came into contact with local traditions and conditions.

The Swedish Rococo was less extreme than its French counterpart and interiors used less surface carving – *boiserie* was usually limited to dadoes – and fewer textiles. Characteristically walls were divided into panels, but these were generally painted to imitate either wainscoting or mouldings, and decorated with painted ornaments. Lighter colours, lighter-hearted *rocaille* motifs and light-reflecting pier glasses, usually with gilded frames, became increasingly popular.

The chief sources of the Rococo were the works of the architects Charles Etienne Briseux and Jacques-François Blondel. Blondel was a central figure in the history of French taste and various editions of his engravings were published between 1737 and (posthumously) 1777, and were followed by other French pattern books, by Briseux in 1743 and by Germain Boffrand in 1745. In these were detailed proposals of everything from façades and ground plans to chimneypieces, door cases, window reveals and even wrought ironwork.

The summer house of the Grill family at Svindersvik, in what is now the eastern suburbs of Stockholm, was the first of the *maisons de plaisance* to be built in the style popularized by Blondel. Designed by Hårleman in the 1740s, the single-storey main building rises to two storeys in the central bay. While the most original and lavish of Hårleman's manor houses was Åkerö, on an island in Lake Yngaren to the south-west of Stockholm, far more influential was his design for the more modest manor at Granhammar, built in 1752. The two-storey rendered stone building had a Mansard roof of painted sheet metal and roofing tiles; the ground plan was rectangular with the *salle* slightly off-set from the main axis.

PREVIOUS PAGES *The brilliant* trompe l'oeil *panels at Åkerö (see page 50) by Johan Pasch, are crowned with maxims from Voltaire, Rousseau and from Åkerö's first owner, Carl Gustaf Tessin.*
RIGHT AND ABOVE *Built in the 1760s from designs by Adelcrantz, the Chinese Pavilion in the gardens of Drottningholm was an idyllic retreat where the royal family could spend the day indulging in hobbies such as wood-turning and embroidery. The characteristically Rococo decoration was based on Chinese motifs seen in François Boucher's engravings, but the artist Pasch interpreted these with a contemporary feel for nature, illustrating pursuits such as gardening and farming, music and games.*

Progressive Refinements

Because it lay unused for most of the nineteenth century, the court theatre at Drottningholm has unusually well-preserved interiors. It was built towards the end of the 1760s – at minimal cost for a queen already in debt – and decorated with wallpapers in c. 1770. Although the paper in this room, known as the Prima Donna's room, was made in Stockholm, its design owes much to the Chinese. The Rococo chest-of-drawers and gilded mirror are listed in the original inventory, but the chairs are Italian of the twentieth century.

Hårleman's designs for houses like Svindersvik and Granhammar were popularized by engravings by Jean Eric Rehn and especially by Carl Wijnblad who, in 1755 published his influential *Architectural Drawings for Forty Domestic Houses of Stone and Thirty of Wood*. This included designs for everything from the smallest log cabin to the grandest stone palace. The 1760s were boom years for house building and Wijnblad's variations on themes by Hårleman and his borrowings from other Swedish as well as foreign

architects helped to spawn the Swedish form of Rococo houses across the length and breadth of the country.

Around this time the white and yellow colours that had become the norm for the façades of stone houses such as Regnaholm also began to appear on wooden houses. One example was Stora Nyckelviken not far from Svindersvik, which was modernized by covering its rough horizontal timbers with dressed vertical boarding. At the same time the lead cames in older windows were often replaced by wooden

The grey mid-eighteenth-century wallpaintings on cloth in the guests' salon on the first floor at Ängsö are decorated with gardenscapes and delicate strings of flowers crowned with yellow ribbons. All are set within trompe l'oeil *frames suggesting gilded wooden mouldings. The dado below has also been skilfully painted to simulate carved grey marble.*

glazing bars, although out in the provinces, the older type of leaded windows continued to be used, and indeed could still be seen in the homes of peasant farmers halfway through the nineteenth century. When the celebrated scientist Carolus Linnaeus was enobled in the 1760s, he acquired a small estate at Hammarby just outside Uppsala, and leaded windows were installed throughout the two-storey wooden house he had built there.

Both inside newly built houses and modernized older properties – such as Ängsö in Västmanland and Sätuna and Åkeshov in Uppland – Rococo elements were adapted according to the means of the owners. The elaborately carved dadoes and mouldings of the panels of the royal palaces were generally interpreted as painted decoration, usually on linen canvas stretched over frames and then fitted to the wall. The engravings of the French court painter François Boucher, especially his Chinese motifs, provided inspiration for murals which were often enhanced with imaginative and ornate frames. A virtuoso of this type of decoration was the immensely productive Johan Pasch, one of the many artists who had worked on the palace in Stockholm, who used Chinese motifs in blue and gold at Sturefors in the 1760s.

A decade earlier Johan Pasch had been commissioned by Count Carl Gustaf Tessin, the son of Tessin the Younger, to decorate the walls of Läckö Castle. The result was highly original: furniture, household utensils and animals appear to be standing in niches or hung on the walls. Twenty or so years later these masterly illusionist panels were moved to one of the wings at Åkerö. This novel idea had few imitators, but word must have slowly spread, for towards the end of the century one of the timber buildings at Ölsboda Manor, in Närke, was decorated with what, at first glance, seems to be a motley assortment of everyday clothes and weapons hung on nails driven into the wall.

Chinoiserie continued to exercise a fascination for most of the century at every level from royalty to *nouveau riche.* The original Chinese Pavilion at Drottningholm was replaced in the 1760s with a far more elaborate one designed by the architect Carl Fredrik Adelcrantz and decorated by Pasch;

in the 1770s the walls of a drawing room at Åkerö were covered with linen panels, framed and painted with Chinese landscapes, while exotic Oriental patterns executed by local painters appear in some small provincial manor houses.

The drawing rooms and state bedrooms of grander houses were still hung with textiles during this period, while dining

rooms were usually wainscoted or had canvas on the walls painted in tones of yellow ochre to resemble panelling. Leather continued to be popular until well into the middle of the century – a house as modern as Granhammar sported gilded leather dining-room walls when it was first built. Elsewhere financial constraints encouraged the development of less extravagant solutions, and paper wallcoverings were a simpler alternative for many interiors. Indeed, the discriminating, if impecunious Queen Louisa Ulrika, used wallpaper for the royal boxes and other rooms regularly used by courtiers at Drottningholm Theatre. The patterns, which were printed from wooden blocks coated with distemper, included boldly patterned stemwork adorned with clusters of leaves as well as flowers, vines and tendrils that clearly drew their inspiration from Chinese or Chinese-inspired French textiles. Made of pieces of paper about 60 centimetres (2 foot) square that were glued together and then pinned or even sewn to the wall, wallpaper enjoyed the greatest popularity in wooden houses, and there are some well-preserved examples at Linnaeus's Hammarby. The textiles used for curtains, bedhangings and upholstery in the grander houses of the Rococo era could be damask, silk or imported Chinese taffeta, painted, or woven in checks, but more often they were cotton or linen printed in simple floral patterns.

While the appeal of Rococo was still largely undiminished in the 1760s, the first signs of a new direction were beginning to appear. The linen panels in the *salle* at Åkerö were painted in the 1750s with vistas through formal gardens framed by columns and Classical sculptures; and at Sturefors, Rehn decorated the Count's study in a restrained scheme of white and gold six years before Pasch had completed his murals of Boucher's light-hearted *chinoiserie* engravings in the Countess's suite in the 1750s. Echoing developments in France in the 1750s, these reactions to the extravagant excesses of Rococo heralded the Neo-Classicism of the Gustavian era.

The walls of the salle *at Sturefors were redecorated towards the end of the 1750s with this host of different marble effects and* faux *mouldings, gilded statues and medallions. The credit for this sumptuous, yet austere effect belongs to the painter Johan Pasch who worked from designs by Rehn. Rehn also provided the designs for the splendid tiled stove emblazoned with the owners' family crest above the mantelshelf. The room itself was built c. 1700 under the aegis of Tessin the Younger.*

Åkerö

ABOVE *Åkerö is set amid beautiful scenery on a sizeable island in Lake Yngaren. Reflecting the Francophile leanings of its owner, the mid-eighteenth-century house was built in accordance with French conventions which dictated that the ground floor had higher ceilings and thus larger windows. The façades have recently been painted with the original colours: cream rendering and pallid red-banded rustication.*

LEFT *One of the walls of the ground-floor* salle *is painted with a formal garden seen in perspective between pairs of Ionic columns and Antique statuary. The illusion of depth is increased by the brightly plumed bird and colourful butterflies in the foreground, while* faux *bas-relief overdoors complete the scheme. The work is that of Olof Fridsberg, and was his first commission at Åkerö when he began the decoration there in 1756. The woodwork and floor – a geometric pattern of black and white marble set in a frieze of grey limestone – were designed by Hårleman, the architect of Åkerö. The symmetry and austerity of the scheme – enhanced by the subtle colour treatment – together with its Classical allusions have led this room to be deemed the first Gustavian-style room.*

The manor house at Åkerö in Södermanland to the south-west of Stockholm was built for Count Carl Gustaf Tessin and his wife, Ulrika Sparre af Sundby. Carl Gustaf trained as an architect like his father and grandfather, but chose to devote his life to politics and the royal court. Thanks to his frequent contacts with the French capital, and the consummate painting skill of Olof Fridsberg, the Count was able to create the most Francophile of all the interiors outside the royal palaces.

Hårleman was commissioned to design the house, and the layout and plans for the façades were finalized towards the end of the 1740s. Inside, the rooms were decorated with an innovative *mélange* of French influences and personal solutions: the painting on the walls in the *salle* recalls the work in Carl Gustaf's childhood home. Other reception rooms were conventionally decorated with walls lined with French silk, while in the more private rooms, such as the Countess's writing room, artistic fantasy was given free rein.

The only items at Åkerö which now remain from Tessin's collections of *objets d'art* are the architectural plans for the house and gardens, and some alternative proposals for decorating the walls of the *salle*. However, Jean Baptiste Oudry's still-lifes recessed into the pier glasses on the upper floor bear witness to the original intentions of the owner and to the splendour with which the house was once decorated.

RIGHT *The walls in the largest room in the north annexe are a* tour de force *of illusionist technique: the intention was to conjure up the impression of a room in use, before the servants had had time to tidy it up! Originally commissioned from Pasch in 1753 for one of the rooms at Läckö Castle in Västergötland, which was also owned by the Tessin family, the panels were moved to Åkerö after Tessin's death in 1770.*

ABOVE *The Countess's writing room was recorded in a gouache painting by Fridsberg who, in 1762, painted the cabinet that stands in the corner. This elaborate visual entertainment which is four metres (thirteen feet) high, was devised by Tessin. It brings together motifs from contemporary French engravings, Oriental figures, a lacquered Chinese cabinet, and a still life. Although he painted directly onto planed pine, Fridsberg has suggested not only the texture and colour of marble and textiles, but also the glistening brilliance of Chinese lacquer. The gouache shows the*

Countess seated at her elegant writing table with her feet on a Turkish prayer mat, the walls behind her hung with painted Chinese silk.

ABOVE *This detail of the top of the corner cabinet is based on an engraving by the French artist, Antoine Coypel, and shows Cupid as a chimney-sweep, holding a hammer to chip off soot. The curtain he is pushing aside hangs on brass rings on an iron pole, just as the curtains would have done at the windows at Åkerö.*

Regnaholm

ABOVE *Built in the early 1760s, Regnaholm still presents an impressive façade to approaching visitors: the main building under a high Mansard roof is flanked by a pair of two-storey detached wings. Most of the mullioned windows have survived intact and the exterior is finished in the same colours as the original scheme.*

LEFT *This ground-floor guest room would have had an open fireplace when it was built; but ten to fifteen years later when the newly invented heat-retaining tiled stoves proved so effective, they were installed in place of the open hearths throughout the house. The green ceramic tiles of this stove were made locally. The colour is pleasingly picked up by the bed and Rococo chairs – all of which still bear their eighteenth-century coats of paint. The bed, whose fabric-covered headboard and canopy are original, dates from 1750; and the walnut chest-of-drawers and the mirror that hangs above it are of a similar date. Although the whitewashed walls would have been covered in wallpaper, the dado – which reaches the height of the window sill – retains its original yellow paint.*

LEFT *Known as the Chinese cabinet, this tiny room takes its name from the oil-painted linen wallcoverings: the exotic motifs reflect the contemporary fascination with a country just beginning to be known in Europe. As gold lacquer would have been too expensive, yellow makes a passing imitation. The wallcovering and the wooden dado, still in its original yellow hue, are typical of the reigning Rococo style. The armchair with its gently curving legs has a yellow gesso finish and a leather seat, and was made in Stockholm during the 1760s or 1770s, while the portraits of Count Bonde and his wife, by the artists David von Krafft and Lucas von Breda, are a generation older.*

RIGHT *The plain plastered walls of Regnaholm's kitchen are painted in their original colours. The turned, white-painted chairs are simpler, Swedish versions of the type of English ladderback chair that was imported to Sweden during the 1720s and 1730s. The work tables arranged against the walls are made of pine and painted in oils. The elegant Rococo sweep of the legs suggests that they may once have been used in the salle before being relegated to service in the kitchen.*

While the estate of Regnaholm lies in the forests of Östergötland, the manor house and stables were built in the early 1760s on a small island in Lake Regnaren that has since been connected to the mainland with a causeway. Axel Wilhelm Gyllenkrok had funds to build a house of such grandeur not only from farming his estates, but also from his small iron foundry. Regnaholm derives much of its special appeal from the beauty of its surroundings: the lake is visible from every main room, and avenues of pollarded trees extend from the house in three directions.

The house was built with bricks from Regnaholm's own brickworks. The ground floor is criss-crossed by corridors leading between the kitchen and scullery, the servants' quarters and six guest suites, while the reception rooms and family's rooms are on the upper floor. Because for most of this century the house has been lived in only during the summer, its interiors have largely escaped modernization. Although few of the original wallcoverings survived the redecoration in the early nineteenth century, the tiled stoves and scrubbed pine floors are in their prime.

BELOW LEFT *The rather ebullient form of this early eighteenth-century sofa in the vestibule at Regnaholm is reminiscent of the Baroque period. Above it hangs a plaque, which once adorned the Swedish Church in Saint Petersburg, commemorating a visit made by Gustav III in his capacity as Count of Gotland to 'this House of the Lord' in 1771.*

BELOW RIGHT *The clock on the upper-floor landing at Regnaholm conceals a musical box, and at one time a tiny organ in the case played melodies every hour on the hour. The dial is signed by Johan Christian Knoop in Stockholm, clockmaker to the royal court. Standing beside it are two dining chairs signed by Carl Magnus Sandberg.*

OPPOSITE *The stairs to the upper floor rise in three flights around a court framed by iron railings and open to the elements. Whitewashed pilaster-strips known as* lesenes *break up the expanse of the light blue walls and here serve as a support for wall sconces, while a dark-blue painted skirting follows the rise of the stairs up to, across and beyond the half-landing.*

Linnaeus's Hammarby

PREVIOUS PAGES *All the decoration and furnishings in the anteroom on the upper floor of Hammarby date from the 1760s when the house was built by Carolus Linnaeus as his summer home. The dado was painted in shades of yellow to resemble wood panels carved with floral ornaments and mussel shells – typical features of the Rococo style. The two portraits by Johan Henrik Scheffel show Linnaeus and his wife, Sara Morea, in their wedding garments in 1739.*

To the left of the gable end of the main building, the turf roof of the east wing and the tiled roof of the west wing can be glimpsed through the foliage. The shutters were screwed in place from the inside when the house was unoccupied.

The front door is reached from a small open porch. The steps lead past agaves in cast-iron containers painted white.

The view over the front garden shows botanically laid-out plants, all carefully labelled. Native Swedish herbs and flowers flourish alongside more exotic flora brought back from foreign parts by Linnaeus's many disciples.

RIGHT ABOVE *The lack of wallcovering on the landing shows clearly the horizontal timbers used in the construction. The simple door made of planks – hiding the stairs to the attic – contrasts with the detail of both the door and frame that lead to the anteroom.*

RIGHT BELOW *Years of soot and smoke have stained the timber walls of the kitchen. Originally, the walls would have been hidden behind rows of shelves holding kitchen utensils and tableware of copper, pewter and wood. These simple wooden tables survive from those days.*

Carolus Linnaeus is probably the best known Swede of all time. His international reputation rests on his introduction of a system of binomial nomenclature for plants which remains the basis of all plant classification today.

In 1754 he acquired the small estate of Hammarby, just outside Uppsala, and four years later built a house there. The main two-storey timber building had a high Mansard roof and, in its ground plan, resembled a latter-day development of the old Swedish *parstuga* or 'double cottage': a single row of rooms leading into one another. It was thus a synthesis of manor house, summer residence and the type of farmhouse whose roots reach back into the Middle Ages.

On a hill behind is a little park with a stone pavilion which once housed Linnaeus's private natural history museum. This remarkable collection, with exhibits from all over the world, is now the property of the Linnean Society in London.

LEFT *It is rare to find the starkly utilitarian simplicity, which was widespread in the town and country homes of royalty, aristocracy and the well-to-do during the eighteenth century, preserved as well and as completely as here at Hammarby. In the absence of any wooden panelling, walls were often painted in a darker hue of grey, red, blue or yellow up to dado level and the level of the window sills, with a lighter one above. In this spartanly decorated room the lower part of the walls is brown while above the yellow dado line they have been spatter painted in pinkish-brown and white.*

PAPAYA *mas. Boerhani. Hæc planta alta erat q*
maturoi die XXX. Januarii

LEFT *Painted on the doorframe leading to Linnaeus's bedroom is the Latin text 'Innocue vivito numen adest', meaning 'Live without blame. God is present'. The walls above the blue-painted dado panelling are covered with a pot-pourri of botanical illustrations published by a friend of his, J.Burmannius. These hand-coloured engravings have inspired artists of our own generation and have formed the basis of modern wallpaper designs. The four-poster bed is hung with cotton fabric printed with an eighteenth-century pattern. The portrait is of Carl Gustaf Tessin, Linnaeus's protector.*

ABOVE *A painting of a whale hangs above the door into Linnaeus's study. The interest in seldom-seen animals and plants was extremely strong in the eighteenth century and the collecting of curiosities was given a new dimension when it was based on serious scientific studies.*

ELEGANCE AND ENLIGHTENMENT

1770 – 1790
The Gustavian style

The supremely elegant style that began to grace the interiors of stately homes in Sweden during the 1770s and early 1780s has long been personally associated with King Gustav III and indeed has come to bear his name. In truth, however, although the King's enthusiastic patronage helped to promulgate it, the style had begun to emerge more than a decade before Gustav's accession in 1771. It was a harmonious marriage between the more mercurial expressions of Rococo frivolity and a new taste for the more restrained forms of Classicism. The result was orderly, almost chaste interiors based on symmetry and pleasing proportions, with an emphasis on the decoration of walls: these were painted to simulate panels and columns, often superimposed by decorative touches such as swags of flowers. While the schemes were light in colour and light in touch, the importance of light itself was emphasized by the use of tall windows, reflective pier glasses and sparkling crystal chandeliers, and was enhanced by plain white ceilings and pale wood floors.

The invention, by Carl Johan Cronstedt and Fabian Wrede in 1767, of the new tiled stoves was to have a major effect upon interiors. Broadly speaking, up until then, it had been practically impossible to occupy a whole suite of rooms during the harsh Swedish winter. Now that changed, transforming social life, and the way in which rooms were used. With their complex system of flues and ducts winding through

heat-retaining bricks, the stoves were up to eight times more efficient as a source of heat than their predecessors. In addition, the fire boxes and front apertures could now be designed on a smaller scale, and the design of the tiles presented almost limitless decorative opportunities. Sales of the stoves soared as their use spread rapidly throughout the country. They replaced open fireplaces and became the focus of the decoration of many Gustavian rooms.

Gustavian Classicism looked to France for inspiration, and the work which perhaps had the greatest significance on its evolution was Jean-François de Neufforge's *Recueil élémentaire d'architecture*. Published in instalments between 1757 and 1770, its innumerable copperplates were a treasure trove of the ornamental motifs – such as laurel wreaths, garlands and medallions – that were to become the hallmarks of the Gustavian style.

Jean Eric Rehn, who was to be the style's chief exponent, was also its pioneer. He had studied engraving in Paris at the Académie des Beaux Arts for five years during the 1740s and then returned to France periodically to acquaint himself with current ideas and to bring back new drawings. Soon after one such visit, and only a year after Neufforge's seminal work first began to appear, Rehn embarked upon the redecoration of the state rooms at the manor house of Sturefors. Using Neufforge's plates as a directory of style, he created what can be seen retrospectively as Sweden's first 'Gustavian' room in

PREVIOUS PAGES *Using the simplest materials – canvas, chalk and glue, and paint – decorative artists working during the 1780s produced wallpaintings of captivating delicacy at Gripsholm Castle (see page 77).*
LEFT AND ABOVE *The decoration at Skogaholm Manor, from Närke (but now re-erected in the museum at Skansen in Stockholm), dates from about 1790 but is quintessentially Gustavian in style. The stretched canvas panels on the walls above the grey dado of this anteroom are painted with Classical ornamentation, such as swags of laurel leaves, in combination with more capricious Rococo motifs in* grisaille, *and there is also an echo of Rococo convention in the overdoor.*

67

Elegance and Enlightenment

Skogaholm has an unusually rich variety of wall panel decoration. The entrance hall has meticulously painted geometric borders embellished with festoons of laurel leaves and bronze-coloured rosettes; one of the bedrooms has a frieze of vines between rows of pearls in grisaille, *a pattern which seems to have been something of a favourite, particularly in the 1790s; and the panels in the main bedchamber have simpler frames with a single string of painted beads.*

BELOW LEFT *Unlike the older four-poster beds, which were completely enshrouded in textile, the beds of the Gustavian period had headboards and footboards in wood and the hangings were relegated to providing frames for the bed-heads. The Classical origins of the carved decoration of this bed are clearly recognizable. The red-brown colour was probably just as common as grey by the 1790s.*

BELOW RIGHT *When Skogaholm was opened as a museum, this room was furnished as a child's room, with miniature copies of full-sized furniture. The simple secrétaire still has its original imitation of walnut or mahogany veneer.*

RIGHT *The salle, seen through the double doors of the hall, was redecorated in 1790 when the Wennerstedt family portraits were set into the white painted panelling. The plaster bust of Gustav III is the work of Johan Tobias Sergel.*

Like most of the tiled stoves at Sturehov, this one, dating from the late 1770s or early 1780s, came from the Marieberg faience factory of Sturehov's owner, Baron Johan Liljencrantz, and is widely regarded as one of the most magnificent ever produced there. The bright colours and perfectly white tiles are the result of a special muffle-kiln process, in which the sensitive glazes are fired in an enclosed chamber and protected from direct contact with the source of the heat. The decoration on the upper part of the stove is centred around the Liljencrantz crest, a shield bearing three fleur-de-lis which is framed in a floral wreath. Above the doors to the fire-box are the Classical images of flaming torches.

This genteel guest room has painted walls divided into panels by slender, sculpted, gilded mouldings, perhaps evidence of the fact that, at some stage in the planning, the intention was to cover the walls with silk. The gilding on the two chairs is a later addition, as is the upholstery fabric.

the Grand Salon at Sturefors. The linen-covered walls were painted to imitate marble, with *faux* niches and moulded frames around portrait medallions, and gilded allegorical sculptures. The laurel wreaths, Greek-key frets, urns and rosettes were typical of what was to be the period's infatuation with Classical forms.

Rehn's other major projects, such as those for Erstavik House in the Stockholm suburbs or the manor house at Gimo in Uppland, owe their layouts to the copperplate engravings of Blondel – which continued to be published through most of the later 1700s – but the special character of the painted walls and the general absence of wood panelling lend them a distinctively Swedish air. The extraordinary integrity of the interiors that Rehn was capable of creating can also be seen at Leufsta and Stora Väsby in Uppland, where he achieved a perfect blend of Classical forms with Rococo ornament. At Leufsta the walls of the dining rooms were decorated with panels marbled in green and blue and crowned with gilded laurel wreaths and Classical cartouches, into which were set family portraits. At Stora Väsby the architraves and panels above the high double doors were painted to simulate the blue-green hues of Sweden's own *kolmården* marble.

Two-storey houses were the norm during the Gustavian period, but Rehn's designs for Erstavik and Forsmark and for his last major project, the manor house at Ljung on the river Motala south-west of Stockholm, show that the last years of the eighteenth century saw a return, on the larger estates, to the three-storey constructions of the seventeenth century. Nevertheless, Ljung, built for Privy Counsellor Fredrik Axel von Fersen some time in the late 1770s, stands today as one of the purest expressions of Gustavian Classicism, and the building itself is probably Sweden's most important monument from this time.

The style's other chief proponent was the Court Architect, Carl Fredrik Adelcrantz, and apart from the work he carried out for the royal family, perhaps his most exemplary achievement was Sturehov, on the shores of Lake Mälaren to the south-west of Stockholm. This was built in 1778 for Gustav III's Minister of Finance, Count Liljencrantz, who was part-owner of the faience factory at Marieberg that manufactured magnificent examples of the new type of ceramic stoves. The distinctive tiles produced there, in bright polychrome designs on a white base, were of unusual clarity and brilliance and have remained objects of admiration ever since. Though many unique stoves were specially commissioned from the factory at Marieberg for the most prominent rooms in manors and castles, most have now been lost; those that do still exist are located in just a few houses, notably Sturehov and nearby Hässelbyholm (which was owned by Liljencrantz's brother).

Both these houses contain some of the finest examples of decorative painting from the Gustavian era, executed by Lars Bolander who had worked on royal commissions at both Ekolsund and Strömsholm, and who is generally considered to be the most accomplished decorative artist of his time. Bolander's exquisite marbling on the panels and walls of the salon and his graceful, unashamedly pretty floral ornamentation in the anterooms are themes which are repeated throughout the houses – even in the bedrooms, for by the 1780s decoratively painted wall panels were beginning to appear in bedrooms, where textile wall hangings had previously been almost obligatory.

Painted linen wall panels were a simple way not only of modernizing interiors but also of breathing charm into otherwise spartan rooms at comparatively low cost. The strings of pearls, garlands of husks and festoons of twining leaves and flowers – often caught up by a bow or ring – that adorn the guests' quarters at Svanå Manor in Västmanland, the Courtiers' Wing at Gripsholm Castle, and the South Wing at Huvudsta Manor just outside Stockholm show how extraordinarily accomplished the decorative painters were at this time.

During the final twenty years or so of the eighteenth century Gustavian Classicism spread far beyond the confines of the royal castles and stately homes of Sweden, and laurel swags, floral festoons and pretty posies of flowers appeared on walls throughout the country. The dissemination – both socially and geographically – of Gustavian wall painting was

Sturehov was built and decorated around 1780 with no expense spared. Everything from the intricate parquet floors to the glittering chandeliers was of sumptuous quality. The view from a bedchamber through the octagonal dining room to an anteroom beyond shows a mixture of contrasting styles: the light-hearted late Rococo floral decoration of the bedroom acts as a foil to the rather uncompromising Classical character of the bronze ornamentation and faux *marbling in the dining room.*

echoed in the proliferation of Gustavian furnishings. This period saw factory production bring printed textiles and faience stoves (and other furnishings such as mirrors and glass) – which had largely been the preserve of royal palaces and stately homes – within reach of a much greater proportion of the population. Export incentives in the form of state subsidies encouraged *ébénistes*, chairmakers, mirror-makers and the makers of clock cases to produce increasingly large series of more or less identical pieces. At the same time, there was a

surge in domestic demand for these products to fill the rooms made usable by the advent of the new tiled stoves, and more and more people wanted furniture such as sofas and armchairs.

Reflecting prevailing taste, furniture gradually acquired more austere lines: the curved Rococo legs of sofas, tables and chairs became simply turned or tapered. Classical ornament such as egg-and-dart motifs, repeated volutes, astragals and Greek key, together with garlands of laurel leaves

The architect of Erstavik, Jean Eric Rehn, provided sketches for the decoration of this anteroom, which was probably carried out within ten years of the house being built in 1765. The canvas panels, painted with Greek-key friezes round delicate blue and white floral designs, play a less important role than usual in this decorative scheme: the accent is rather on the painted wainscoting of the walls, the garlanded overdoors and the pair of moulded double doors. The unpainted pine floorboards are laid in a simple, elegant pattern.

appeared, carved or moulded, on beds, chair rails and backrests. The most-copied Gustavian chair has a medallion back, upholstered seat with rounded corners, turned legs and is decorated with carved stylized flowers at the top of the front legs and top of the medallion. The wood sofa that we now think of as typically Gustavian – with straight back and side panels and loose squabs – derived from much earlier English upholstered sofas. At the same time the most popular colour for chairs, sofas and beds changed from the light yellow favoured during the 1760s and 1770s to a subtle shade of grey, applied as an oil-based paint rather than the Rococo's layers of gesso colours.

Just as painted canvases replaced silk wallcoverings, so printed cotton calico began to take over the role of silk in loose furnishings. It was often waxed to resemble silk and was known as *sits* or *sitzer* cloth. For normal domestic use, however, home-woven linens in striped and checked designs – blue or red, always in conjunction with white – remained the cheapest alternative. Commonly encountered in provincial manor houses as bed hangings, wallcoverings and furniture upholstery, they could also be seen in royal residences, although there they were used merely as protective loose covers on the grand upholstery, or in the more simple rooms of the servants' quarters. Checked designs were also used for more expensive fabric, particularly taffeta, and were made into curtains and upholstery in grander situations.

The overriding need to make the most of light was met during the Gustavian era by tall windows which were often dressed with delicate, thin white cotton curtains caught up in festoons and swags, often held in place above the windows with rosettes in a contrasting colour. These were used in conjunction with roller blinds, pulled down to protect the interiors from the bleaching effects of sunlight. Light was then maximized by white plastered ceilings and pale colour schemes, by elaborate brass and crystal chandeliers, and by the introduction of gilded mirrors. Whether these were set in simple beading or richly carved frames, wall mirrors and mirror candle-sconces brought elegance, light and a feeling of spaciousness to Gustavian rooms.

BELOW *Sven Liljencrantz, the County Governor, installed new tiled stoves from his brother Johan's renowned Marieberg faience factory at Hässelbyholm and this is one of the few that survive, still standing on the original wooden feet. The door on the right is a design that was introduced by Hårleman during the 1740s. Divided into three panels, the highest and lowest with an extra moulding, it remained the standard for reception-room doors until superseded by double doors at the end of the century.*

RIGHT *Built in the
mid-seventeenth century,
Hässelbyholm Manor in
Södermanland was renovated
in the late 1770s and early
1780s at which time the
canvas wall panels were
painted with consummate
artistry by Lars Bolander.
The* trompe l'oeil *laurel leaf
border echoes the carved
decoration on the top of the
Gustavian sofa.*

Gripsholm

ABOVE *Around 1780 Gustav III had a new wing added along the north side of the outer courtyard of the red-brick medieval castle of Gripsholm. It looks from the outside like a double-storey building. However, the two rows of tall windows hide an architectural secret: it is, in reality, a four-storey construction.*

LEFT *The twenty-eight almost identical guest rooms in what has come to be known as the Courtiers' Wing were decorated in c.1780. Sparsely but elegantly furnished, they convey a very good idea of the contemporary decorative ideals. The walls were covered in canvas panels depicting softly curling tendrils of flowers and foliage or garlands of corn husks framed by* faux *mouldings. Each room has a stove covered in tiles that range from monotone grey and shimmering green to cobalt blue repeat patterns of flower-draped urns or cartouches. Each room also has its own textile pattern repeated in the bed hangings and upholstered panels of the headboard and footboard.*

The guest rooms of the new wing at Gripsholm were designed for the courtiers' gentlemen and ladies-in-waiting. The men's quarters were more austere than the women's and where the ladies had 'Gripsholm' armchairs (*bergères* with loose squabs in the seat and back), the gentlemen had simpler dining chairs with oval wooden backs and pierced splats. So appealing are the wallpaintings that it is difficult to imagine that in the middle of the nineteenth century, when factory-made wallpapers were held in greater esteem than handpainted schemes, many were simply papered over. At the turn of the century, however, artists like Carl Larsson and the architect Fredrik Liljekvist, who led the restoration of Gripsholm, rediscovered the merits of Gustavian decor, and since then numerous furniture and textile manufacturers and interior designers have launched various versions of eighteenth-century domestic furnishings, all relying heavily on those in the Courtiers' Wing guest rooms at Gripsholm.

RIGHT *All the beds in the Courtiers' Wing are set in shallow alcoves framed by profiled mouldings and hung with printed calico curtains and pelmets. Adjacent to the alcoves are small built-in wardrobes. It is not only the furnishings that have survived, but also the mattresses, pillows and quilts, which are all marked with a number denoting the room for which they were originally intended. The only thing that has changed significantly over the past two hundred years is that cotton gingham has replaced the original wool shag upholstery on the chairs.*

LEFT *The delicacy with which the wall panels were painted, and especially the addition of birds and butterflies, owed much to the prevailing influence of Chinese painting.*

Svindersvik

ABOVE *Svindersvik occupies a patch of high ground overlooking a bay of the Saltsjön Sea on the eastern approaches to Stockholm. Seen through the main gates from the orchard, the house looks imposing; it is, in fact, a very small single-storey building with a grand, pedimented two-storey bay in the centre. The rendered façades have been repainted in the original colour scheme of red, yellow and white.*

LEFT *Some time around 1780, just over thirty years after Svindersvik was built, the original two rooms to the left of the entrance hall were combined to make a single large anteroom which was redecorated with pier glasses and delicately hand-painted wallpaper imported from China. Though a Rococo flavour still pervades the decoration, the furniture has been added to by generations of families who continued to use Svindersvik until well into the 1940s as well as by its current owner, the Nordic Museum in Stockholm. The early nineteenth-century armchairs, signed 'Jacob of Paris', have the loose covers which were customary in Sweden to protect the fine silk from the effects of direct sun.*

Svindersvik was built in the late 1740s to plans by Carl Hårleman, the Court architect, as a summer retreat for Claes Grill, who was a factory owner and director of the Swedish East India Company. Some forty years later, it was bought by an extremely wealthy widow, Catharine Charlotta Ribbing, who redecorated and added a timber extension to one of the annexes, supposedly to entertain King Gustav III. Known as the Svindersvik Pavilion, this annexe is an exceptionally well-preserved example of Gustavian decoration.

RIGHT ABOVE *One of the guest rooms in the Pavilion was decorated in the 1780s with painted canvases that extend from the ceiling's cavetto mouldings down to the skirting boards. The effect is one of a panelled dado up to window sill height, above which yellow panels are surrounded by gilded* trompe l'oeil *frames and yellow and white borders.*

The silk damask bed hangings echo the colour of the walls, reflecting the taste for harmonious colour schemes. The bed, which dates from the 1740s, is a simple wooden construction, and can be made into a double bed by pulling out the long side. A so-called 'lit à la polonaise', its tester is embellished with a gilded dragon.

RIGHT BELOW *Symmetry was one of the most dominant aesthetic expressions of eighteenth-century design: thus when the vestibule of the Pavilion was redecorated in the 1780s, a wooden replica was installed at the same time as the columnar tiled stove, the walls above the dado were finished with identical distempered canvases, and a folding serving table was placed on each side of the doors. While the glazed tiles on the stove have retained their original colour and lustre, the oil paint on the wooden replica – used as a storage cupboard – has faded.*

BELOW LEFT *While the woodwork and painted linen* chinoiserie *wall panels of the master bedroom reveal the house's Rococo pedigree, the furniture dates from around 1790. Flying half-tester beds like this were first seen in Sweden in the 1780s. The chairs have loose covers to protect the valuable silk beneath.*

BELOW RIGHT *The anteroom outside the bedroom in the main building has a plaster ceiling painted to resemble swallows flying in the open sky. Above the grey wood dado, yellow canvases imitate the traditional Rococo pale wood panelling. The walnut-veneered* secrétaire *and the chairs date from* c. *1790.*

OVERLEAF *The dividing line between theatrical decor and domestic interior design was a tenuous one during the Gustavian era and the airy Grand Salon in the Pavilion has all the showiness of a stage setting. Ionic pilasters and vertical panels hint at the new taste for Neo-Classicism that was just beginning to make itself felt: the images were inspired by Raphael's frescoes in the Vatican and by the new archaeological discoveries from Pompeii and Herculaneum. It was the excavations of Antique Classical sites that spawned the term 'grotesques' (from the word grottoes) to describe the type of delicate ornamentation seen in the panels.*

Sörby

ABOVE *The manor house at Sörby stands in the lush green countryside around Lake Mosjön in Närke. The original single-storey log building was painted Falu red and had a façade that was only four windows wide. Some time in the mid-nineteenth century, however, the size of the house was doubled, an extra storey added and the whole construction panelled and painted white.*

LEFT *The walls of the* salle *are panelled up to the height of the window sills with horizontal boards. Above them the canvas panels are decorated in the contemporary fashion of 1780-85 with painted garlands of laurel leaves and ribbons. At some later juncture, probably around the middle of the nineteenth century, the canvas was covered with slate-blue paint and the woodwork was painted white. The work involved in removing both these coats of paint has now started. The 1790s armchair is a later development of the type of chair with loose seat and back squabs that was introduced into Sweden in the middle of the eighteenth century.*

When the late seventeenth-century manor house of Sörby was acquired between 1780 and 1785 by the Court Chaplain, Erik Waller, he set about modernizing the interiors. His familiarity with the latest styles in decoration can perhaps be explained by his fond interest for fashion in general: Waller had earlier been awarded the gold medal of the Royal Patriotic Society for his contribution to the creation of a Swedish national costume. At Sörby, many of the rooms were decorated with designs straight out of contemporary pattern books.

Unfortunately a wholesale renovation during the nineteenth century disguised much of the Gustavian decoration. However, having been abandoned for some twenty years, the house is now being carefully restored. The nineteenth-century extension has already been demolished, revealing the original red timbers of the exterior, and the roof is once more restored to its *säteri* silhouette.

LEFT *The anteroom at one end of the house has the same horizontally boarded dado as the other rooms. The wall panels are decorated with swags and tails of roses and sea-green foliage. The clock, which dates from the 1780s, is of a type that first appeared in Stockholm during the Rococo period. Now referred to as Mora clocks – from the town in the province of Dalarna where they were produced until the mid-nineteenth century – their voluptuous curves proved particularly popular in rural areas. Seen through the door is the entrance hall whose glass-panelled doors lead to the porch.*

RIGHT *The ceiling of this small bedroom is finished in white plaster, while the walls are fitted, as elsewhere in the house, with delicately painted canvases. Most of the white paint on the three-panelled door and the doorframe has been removed to reveal the original grey oil paint beneath. The Gustavian-style bed is extendable: when not in use, it could be pushed together to only half its length, a distinct advantage in the often cramped living conditions of the time.*

1790 - 1820
The influence of Neo-Classicism and the French Empire

URBANE

SOPHISTICATION

Gustav III's journey to Italy during 1783-4 gave impetus to a new direction in interior decoration in Sweden. Partly as a reaction to the perceived frivolity and excesses of the Rococo, and stimulated by archaeological discoveries from the lava-entombed cities of Pompeii and Herculaneum, a renewed interest in the Classical civilizations was beginning to make its mark on European interiors. Tiled stoves now assumed the forms of sacrificial altars or Classical columns, for example, and the mouldings round ceilings and panels developed new profiles based on Greek patterns such as the ovolo with egg-and-dart decoration. The buildings of ancient Greece and Rome had been the subject of study and admiration since the middle of the previous century, but what distinguished Neo-Classicism from the Baroque was a concern for stylistic correctness and purity. In addition, the publication, during the 1770s, of treatises based on first-hand observation of the Antique brought accurate information to a far wider audience for the first time. Italy made a strong impact on Gustav and he returned to Sweden full of ideas for new projects. He brought with him the architect Louis Jean Desprez. Desprez, along with the interior designer and decorative painter Louis Masreliez, was French; both were to play a major part in the spread of the new style. The most extravagant expression of the King's new predilections was to be the palace at Haga, conceived as a gigantic, domed centrepiece reminiscent of the Pantheon, to be flanked by vast arcaded wings. These grandiose plans, however, never came to fruition, but the new style can be seen in the pavilion that was rebuilt to house the King while work on the main palace was carried out.

Designed by architect Olof Tempelman, the Haga Pavilion, originally of wood, extended with brick and stone and subsequently rendered, had an Italianate flat roof crowned with a balustrade. Due to the exigencies of the Swedish climate however, this feature had few imitators and most architects of the time preferred low pitched roofs. Inside, the magnificent Pompeian interiors, executed in the late 1780s, were chiefly the responsibility of Masreliez. The dining room feigns the cool, austere character of stone, but the decoration and furnishings of the other rooms are positively sumptuous. In addition to the illusionist painted ornamentation, gilded 'pastellage' mouldings were used for doors, panel frames and furnishings. Pastellage, which used a malleable, gesso-like blend of chalk and oil, was to prove a time-saving way of producing richly decorated, small-scale repeating patterns, such as the Classical Greek egg-and-dart, cording, or stylized acanthus foliage. Although splendour like this was not matched outside the royal court, the Pompeian nature of the painted decorations was to be much imitated. One of the earliest examples can be seen in the Classical borders and friezes at Bernshammar in Västmanland.

The painted borders round canvas wall panels in this style

PREVIOUS PAGES *The paper cornice of archetypal Classical Greek mouldings, and the dramatic* trompe l'oeil
wall panel including two Dionysian staffs were highly fashionable when they were painted at Broby in c.1815.
ABOVE *A painted roundel in the moulded framework edging the canvas wall panels in the Grand Salon
in the pavilion at Haga shows Cupid at the plough.*
RIGHT *The dining room of the pavilion at Haga, religiously restored in the 1940s, is an embodiment of what has
become known as 'the stone style'. The plastered walls are painted to suggest features such as Corinthian pilasters
and bas-relief friezes, while the metal stove presides over the room from a* trompe l'oeil *niche.*

were to enjoy widespread popularity for some length of time. They were considered the height of fashion when they appeared at Ekensberg on Lake Mälaren, in 1795, and were still just as up-to-date in 1804 when David Gotthard Hildebrand, a man of considerable means, replaced the silk on the walls of Nynäs Manor with painted decor.

Marbling and stone effects continued to be popular, especially for dining rooms. The walls of the dining room of what is now known as Haga Palace (the villa-like annexe erected adjacent to the pavilion at Haga as a home for the royal children) were marbled in grey and white panels, edged with yellow borders. Perhaps the finest marbling of this period is to be found at Krusenberg on Lake Mälaren.

The effect of sumptuous, corded and tassled drapery on walls became extremely fashionable towards the turn of the century, and was still in vogue as the 1820s drew to a close. This form of decorative painting first appeared in its Neo-Classical guise at Bernshammar around 1790 and the walls of the anterooms and bedrooms at Haga Palace were finished in this fashion with distemper paint about 1805, though all traces of this original decoration have long since disappeared. Fortunately the green *trompe l'oeil* swags of drapery which were painted on paper, probably between 1810 and 1820, have been preserved at Broby Manor in Södermanland. In the late 1820s, the magnificent salon at Skottorp in Halland on Sweden's west coast was painted with draped red silk below painted imitations of Classical bas-relief friezes.

By this time *trompe l'oeil* drapes were being printed on paper in sections in France and imported to Sweden, where

ABOVE *A detail from one of the walls of an anteroom in the Haga Pavilion shows the exquisite workmanship of the Pompeian-inspired scheme. While it bears a marked resemblance both to Robert Adam's 1760s pattern-work in England and to the interiors of palaces such as Fontainebleau, carried out in France in the 1770s and 1780s, Masreliez's mélange of painted grotesques and wood-and-pastellage panelling, which was completed in the late 1780s, is now recognized as the summit of Swedish Neo-Classicism.*

RIGHT *The Divan Room at Bernshammar, which takes its name from the Turkish-style sofas, was decorated in 1787-8, by Anders Zettergren and Per Emanuel Limnell, both of whom had worked at the Stockholm Opera. The elegant Pompeian wall decoration on the pilasters and panel frames includes Zodiac symbols and medallions based on blue-and-white Wedgwood china (which itself took its inspiration from Etruscan excavations). Divans were regarded as extremely chic in the 1780s; they were often fixed in place and could take up one, two or even three walls.*

LEFT *The lavish green silk drapery with black, gold and white borders was painted at Broby in c.1815 under the aegis of Carl Christoffer Gjörwell, the leading interior designer of his day. This type of wall decoration, either painted by hand or cut from printed sheets, was introduced around 1800, and soon proved to be a relatively inexpensive way of keeping pace with changing fashions. One of the sources may have been Krafft and Ransonette's studies of French interiors from the 1790s, which first appeared in 1802.*

RIGHT *These anterooms at Nynäs Manor were renovated around 1790 and given new panelling, double doors, pier glasses and chests-of-drawers with mahogany veneer. The floors were carefully finished with a golden-brown oil paint to resemble parquet flooring. In 1804, the fifteen-year-old silk damask wallcoverings were replaced by canvases decorated with Classical borders in shades of apricot pink and duck-egg green to match the overdoors.*

they appeared chiefly as borders, friezes and overdoors, providing a simple solution to the obligations of decorating in the new French style. At the same time, printed paper impressions of textiles were beginning to be used – as they were in one of the newly decorated rooms at Ekensberg – in rooms that would previously have been painted by hand. French-made panoramic wallpaper was also imported during the early 1800s and was eagerly acquired, particularly by the *nouveaux riches*. With their colourful landscape scenes, these wallpapers were usually displayed in anterooms.

So popular was painted decoration during the Late Gustavian period that it began to appear on floorboards. Some bare pine or spruce floorboards were painted with patterns to imitate oak parquet, others to mimic the elaborate patterns of wall-to-wall carpets. Several of the rooms on the main floor at Ekensberg have floors tinted yellowish-brown with intersecting black and brown lines added to feign the appearance of oak parquet laid in a lozenge pattern, while others have been stencilled with red and green stars or petals at regular intervals over the floor to give the impression of a patterned carpet. The floors at Bernshammar were either painted yellow-brown all over or, as in what used to be the master bedroom, edged with ornamental borders of painted foliage. This form of decorative work was largely reserved for the reception rooms and the guest rooms of grander houses, while scrubbed deal floors remained very much the norm in the day rooms and in less ostentatious homes.

The size and complexity of the curtain arrangements surpassed the elaborate swags of drapery painted on the walls so that they were occasionally works of art in themselves. Curtains were often hung in double rows, either in a single colour chosen to harmonize or contrast with the colours of the walls and furnishing fabrics, or perhaps in white with accoutrements in varying shades. Meanwhile, the window-panes and the windows themselves of new homes tended to be larger in the early 1800s.

Many of the furnishings, furniture and stoves of this era owed much to the lines and design of the altars, sarcophagi and plinths of ancient Greece and Rome, and to the bronze furniture excavated from the volcanic ash of Herculaneum and Pompeii. Pier glasses, which continued to be widely popular, frequently bore crests held aloft by colonnades, or by caryatids, or pillars terminating in heads or busts sometimes referred to as 'herms'. The most fashionable light sources, the *torchères* or candle-stands, were inspired by Antique marble candelabra. These were often made of giltwood or carved wood painted to resemble gilded or

LEFT AND BELOW *Decorated shortly before 1810, the salon at Ramnäs is Empire in feeling with its stylized motifs and bright colours. The blue walls are crowned with painted fringed and tasselled festoons of drapery held aloft by golden shields* (peltas) *and trophies. A pier glass is set in the wall above the gilded, polished-granite fireplace, while the rest of the chimneypiece is a grisaille representation of Classical motifs.*

patinated bronze, and decorated with pastellage.

Klismos chairs with curved back and legs and 'tub' chairs and sofas in Pompeian style with cloven feet and overstuffed upholstery came into vogue as did a new type of sofa, the high-armed divan, which made its debut in the 1780s. The seat and front rail were covered with textiles finished in tassels and fringes, while the loose back cushions were often in a contrasting colour. Special reception rooms furnished with divans, sometimes fitted to the walls, sometimes elegantly rounded, were installed both in the royal palaces and in some

of the more affluent homes, where they came to be known as 'divan rooms'.

By this time the tiled stoves invented by Cronstedt and Wrede had proved that taller models, which forced the smoke to negotiate a series of channels and ducts before rising up through the chimney, produced more heat. However, even though they generated less heat, the almost obsessive worship of Classical Antiquity dictated the building of low stoves, in order that they could act as plinths for the ubiquitous urns and sculptures. These types of stove were usually clad in monochrome white or grey tiles.

Inspiration for contemporary buildings such as the cupola-crowned vestibule of the library at Ekebyholm of 1801, or the early nineteenth-century rotunda at Broby in Södermanland also came from Classical sources. However, the most common type of house of this period was a strictly rectilinear, two-storey building boasting a pitched roof – such as Ramnäs Manor in Västmanland, built in *c.* 1800, which has granite columns flanking the main portal – and was a type of house that served as a model for the homes of the aspirant rural propertied classes during the nineteenth century.

The interior decoration of both Ramnäs and Broby, with their plain, unpanelled brightly coloured walls, painted draped silks, heavy curtains and floor-to-ceiling pier glasses points the way towards the Empire style. Named after the Imperial phase of Napoleon's career, and developed in France, this style coincided with a new dynasty in Sweden. Jean Baptiste Bernadotte, a Frenchman, was adopted as heir to the throne in 1810 and acceded under the name of King Carl XIV Johan in 1818. By that time not only books but magazines were being devoted to interior design, so that new ideas spread rapidly through Europe. Katthamra on the island of Gotland in the Baltic has fine examples of the advanced Empire style from the period around the 1820s and 1830s, including pairs of double doors, tall monochrome tiled stoves and bright colours. Its painted friezes and drapery were the last vestiges of the Late Gustavian tradition before industrially produced rolls of wallpaper began to oust the decorative artist from interior design in the middle of the century.

Ekensberg

ABOVE *Ekensberg rises above a terraced formal garden as if it were a Roman villa somehow transported to the shores of Lake Mälaren. The Italianate appearance of the house was even more pronounced before the balustrade on the roof was removed in the nineteenth century.*

LEFT *Seen from the drawing room is the enfilade of light-suffused reception rooms. Fifteen years after the completion of the house, this room was redecorated: it was given printed French wallpaper and a pair of low white-tiled 'postament' stoves which, like pagan altars for offerings, became plinths for sculptures – here an alabaster group by Johan Tobias Sergel, a leading Gustavian sculptor. By the window is Sergel's scale model of a bronze statue of Gustav III, and on the console table in the room beyond is a copy of Sergel's sculpture of Cupid and Psyche. The base on which the sculpture of Gustav III stands resembles porphyry, but is really spatter-painted wood. The high double doors with their surface-mounted brass locks were innovative at the time. An oval medallion carries a profile of the architect Carl August Ehrensvärd who, in the 1790s, designed garden follies for his cousin, at that time the owner of Ekensberg.*

The three-storey manor house of Ekensberg in rendered brick is unusual, firstly since it was one of the few large commissions undertaken during the Russian-Swedish war of 1788-90, but also because of its striking affinity to an Italian Renaissance villa, a testament to the Neo-Classical style that took Sweden by storm after King Gustav III's return from Italy in 1784. The house was built for the County Governor, Michael von Törne, and his father-in-law, Marshal of the Realm, Count Gustav Adolf Hjärne. The roof was originally sheathed in copper, a rare and expensive material in those days; it is now clad in iron. Contemporary accounts vouch that the interior decoration was in 'the very latest taste'. After

years of mismanagement, work has now commenced on a long-term renovation process. This has been greatly helped by an inventory that was made in the mid-1790s, shortly after the building work had been completed, from which we know how each of the rooms was furnished, and even what textiles were used in the upholstery.

The painstaking work of exposing the original colours on the walls is gradually providing an insight into the true qualities of late eighteenth-century design, albeit in worn and dilapidated form. One of the main principles behind this renovation project, which may never be fully realized, is to leave these older coats of paint as they are, no matter how worn they may be.

OPPOSITE *A late eighteenth-century sofa which served as the model for the newly produced sofa in IKEA's series of eighteenth-century furnishings.*

LEFT *Dating from 1795, the original Gustavian wall decoration, painted on canvas, was revealed after layer upon layer of wallpaper and newspaper had been removed. When the house was acquired by its current owners in the mid-1970s, there was no heating in this room. However, the limestone floor tiles bore traces of a type of ceramic stove with tapering, fluted wooden legs, that has now been installed. The smoking urn detail shows that by 1790 not even stovemakers could disregard the all-pervasive influence of Neo-Classicism.*

The broad floorboards, of spruce and pine, were originally painted in shades of golden-brown and dark brown to imitate light oak parquet. The panels, dado, and high double doors, were painted light grey, while the plaster ceiling and coving were whitewashed.

The furniture typifies the Gustavian ideals: a three-drawer mahogany-veneered console from 1789, complete with its natural stone top and a simple painted armchair.

LEFT *The pattern on a tiled stove may consist of a single motif, such as this diagonal floral ribbon device, repeated on all the flat tiles.*

RIGHT *The top-floor rooms are simply decorated: above the pearl-grey dado the walls are painted in yellow, pink, green or blue.*

The principle indicator of Gustavian design is the faience stove. Although its rectangular shape, deep fire box, post-formed mantelshelf and slim chimney date from the 1740s, it was in fact produced much later. The decorative design on the tiles, however, was little affected by technological progress – this Chinese-inspired motif was first drawn by Jean Eric Rehn decades earlier.

Among the original furnishings which have now been returned to Ekensberg is the white-painted chair. Its simple design suggests that it probably came from the servants' quarters or one of the guest rooms. The blue-and-white-painted sofa has no back and is sometimes described as a divan with loose cushions against the wall. The four-poster bed has a valance of calico printed in an eighteenth-century design.

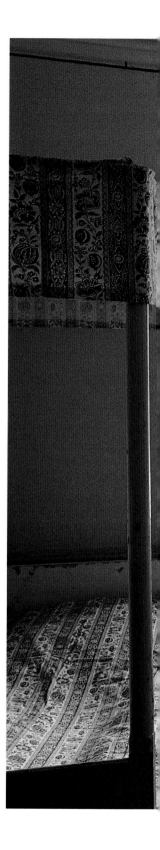

Almare-Stäket

ABOVE *The main entrance of Almare-Stäket, on one of the gable ends, is in the style of a Classical temple: austere granite columns hold up a plain architrave and frieze, and the pitched roof has been made to resemble a pediment decorated with small square mutules.*

RIGHT *The salon at Almare-Stäket is one of the most lavishly decorated late Gustavian rooms. The delicately painted wall canvases were long thought to have been destined for Gustav III's palace at Haga. In reality they were not produced until the early 1800s, by which time Gustav IV already occupied the throne. The chandelier and the white-tiled stove with its gilt trim also date from the early 1800s, even though they are reminiscent of late eighteenth-century models.*

In 1801 the new owner of Almare-Stäket, Samuel af Ugglas, had the original sixteenth-century house on the shores of Lake Mälaren remodelled to a design by Gustav Albrecht Pfeffer. The result included some of the period's most up-to-date interiors.

Samuel af Ugglas was the Governor of Stockholm and had the King to thank for his success: for this reason he stipulated that a bust of the King – who was assassinated in 1792 – should be kept in the house for all time in memory of him.

The house is still owned by the same family who have kept the early nineteeth-century decoration and furniture much as it was – including the bust of Gustav III which presides over the salon.

This dignified bedchamber is one of a suite of guest rooms. The contrast between the deep red silk that covers the bed and divan and the bright green distempered wallpaper is typical of the era's fondness for such juxtapositions. The details of the blue and gold border of palmettes beneath the simple cored cornice, the blue and gold motifs on the stove and the paper frames of the engravings are clearly derived from Graeco-Roman sources.

Pasting copperplate engravings on monochrome walls had been an established decorative device since the 1750s (Carl Gustaf Tessin, for example, had decorated his wife's apartment in the Hessenstiernska Palace in Stockholm in this manner), but it became highly fashionable in the 1780s and 1790s, after Gustav III had used the technique to decorate one of the rooms in the Royal Palace with engravings by Piranesi.

Katthamra

Katthamra is one of the few real manor houses on Gotland, and is the island's largest, most imposing residence. Its original owners' wealth was based on the limestone kilns that have been producing building lime for the mainland since the seventeenth century. In 1805 the estate was taken over by Axel Hägg whose family added a second storey to the house and redecorated it in the early part of the nineteenth century. The house remained in the same family's keeping until the 1930s which explains why many of the interiors are so well-preserved.

PREVIOUS PAGES *Even though its strictly symmetrical façade and Mansard roof give the impression that Katthamra is Rococo in style, the upper floor was not, in fact, added until 1812. At that time a statue of the goddess Diana, which probably dates from the seventeenth century, was placed above the front door.*

The interiors on the upper floors were decorated in the Empire style, but the effects were created solely on paper. All the details depicted are typical of the era's obsession with the Antique: smoking urns, statues in niches, quivers with bows and arrows, elaborately swagged drapery and the head of Mercury, as well as the trompe l'oeil *architectural overdoor with its corbels and pediment. The flush dado with a simply profiled surbase is typical of the period. The interiors are an example of the kind of time-lag that existed in Sweden between the espousal of a new style or trend in the capital and its arrival in the outer reaches of the country. Most of the ideas adopted at Katthamra when it was enlarged and redecorated in the late 1820s – or even 1830s – had been current in Stockholm at the turn of the century.*

LEFT AND RIGHT *Countless variations* of trompe l'oeil draped textiles adorned the walls of the great houses during the Empire period. This particular design, purporting to be simple pull-up blinds beneath tasselled muslin festoons, was hand-painted directly on paper and is in an upper-floor bedroom. The tiled stove, whose greyish-white hues were presumably meant to suggest marble, is of a type that was first seen shortly before 1790 in the Haga Pavilion, and continued to be in production throughout the first quarter of the nineteenth century: the columnar chimney rests on an altar-like plinth and the tiled base extends to the floor.

SPAS AND

*Holiday homes
on lakeshores
and islands*

SUMMER HOUSES

The Swedish custom of spending the summer months at a seaside cottage or perhaps even a house of one's own in the country, may seem to be a typical consequence of the statutory holidays introduced in our own century. However, for the ruling classes of Sweden, retiring to simple homes or to pavilions set in their own parks has been one of summer's pleasures since the Renaissance. Nevertheless, it was not until the first half of the eighteenth century that both the nobility and the burghers acquired a taste for the *malmgård*, a weekend home situated in its own grounds on the outskirts of town, often complete with kitchen and ornamental gardens. The modest summer house of the Grill family at Svindersvik (see page 81), with its magnificent location on the shores of the Saltsjön Sea, was built very much as part of the fashion for an out-of-town *malmgård*, and by the 1740s similar houses and folly-like structures known as 'vanities' were beginning to line the bluffs of Södermalm, to the south of Stockholm.

A belief in the benefits of country and sea air was echoed in the popular interest in the therapeutic qualities of mineral springs, and spas such as those at Medevi, Porla, Ramlösa, and Loka were at their most popular during the eighteenth and nineteenth centuries. The attractions that brought the *beau monde* flocking to Medevi were not only the waters themselves which were rich in iron and considered a cure for, among other things, infertility. The spa held another appeal, for it was to Medevi that the royal family and the court would occasionally retreat to relax in modest surroundings. The web of political intrigue that was so much a part of the Age of Freedom could be spun almost unnoticed under the cover of 'taking the waters', and the opportunities that the spas offered for broadening one's circle of acquaintances with an eye, perhaps, to marriage or business, was another factor that contributed to their popularity. Some of the houses built at the spas were new timber constructions, others were moved there, having served as wings or even the main buildings of other country manors. In many respects a spa like Medevi resembled nothing so much as an eighteenth-century equivalent of today's camp-sites with their retinue of caravans.

In the early years of the nineteenth century the ripples of the social upheaval which followed in the wake of the French Revolution spread as far as Sweden, and power shifted to manufacturers and businessmen, who were keen to consolidate their positions and demonstrate their wealth in building second, summer homes. At the same time, the development of steam-powered ships meant that, from about 1830, Stockholm was within easy reach of the summer residences that dotted the shores of Lake Mälaren to the west or studded the islands and skerries in the archipelago to the east. Meanwhile, the steady transition of housing in the towns and cities from clusters of wooden buildings, each with its own patch of garden, to barrack-like tenements, made the open-air life seem

PREVIOUS PAGES *The view from a fretwork-decorated terrace at Gransäter overlooking one of the many peaceful stretches of water in the Stockholm archipelago.*
LEFT *The unselfconscious fusion of styles – everything from Neo-Romantic Viking architecture to contemporary European Art Nouveau – that marked the summer homes of the bourgeoisie in the late nineteenth century is seen here at Gransäter. The house was designed between 1887 and 1897 by Agi Lindegren for the art historian John Böttiger at a time when the arts, underpinned by a firm belief in the future, flourished as rarely before.*
ABOVE *Visitors to Gransäter are welcomed by the simple message: 'May the peace of God be with you'.*

ABOVE *Like many late-nineteenth-century summer homes in the Stockholm archipelago, this brightly painted house is decorated with exuberant 'gingerbread' woodwork. Ground-floor verandas were frequently glazed and often boasted extra detail in the mullions, while upper verandas were generally open to the elements.*

OPPOSITE, RIGHT *Known locally as 'Queen Christina's Pavilion', this eighteenth-century belvedere at Stallmästargården close to the Haga park north of Stockholm is one of Sweden's oldest.*

OPPOSITE, FAR RIGHT *The rather austere lines of this bathing house on the island of Skarpö in the Stockholm archipelago are borrowed from late-seventeenth-century architecture. It was built in the early years of the twentieth century when Swedish art and literature were steeped in nationalism, and this trend also left its mark in the architecture and interior design – seen in a marked increase in the use of traditional Swedish materials, such as tar and roofing shingles, or, as on the roof illustrated here, overlapping tarred planks.*

LEFT *This gazebo perched on a stone-walled promontory at Lidingö, just outside Stockholm, was built towards the end of the nineteenth century when architectural silhouettes were chosen with impunity, and Neo-Romantic Viking styles rubbed shoulders with Swiss chalets, Moorish follies, and fantastic confections from Turkey and the Far East. The choice could be made from pattern books or from illustrations of pre-fabricated designs advertised in newpapers and journals.*

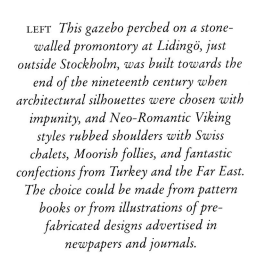

LEFT *This octagonal pavilion of 1888 at Gustavslund, north-east of Stockholm, shows the period's love of Romantic style and its fascination for modern technology: complex glazing bars enclose panes of sand-blasted glass.*

OPPOSITE *A new lifestyle, promoting cold-water bathing, was the reason for the proliferation of wooden bathing houses of every shape and size in the second half of the nineteenth century. At the same time verandas assumed the role of modern reception rooms.*

NEAR RIGHT *The austerity of Classical stonework has been translated into the wooden pillars supporting the joists above a veranda at Bönan, near Gävle in Gästrikland.*

CENTRE *The bathing hut on the promontory of Hasseludden was built in 1860 in the form of a Classical temple to Neptune – the sea god's trident stands on the apex of the roof.*

FAR RIGHT *Old Norse techniques mingle with Classical and Islamic features in the late nineteenth-century woodwork of a veranda on Lidingö Island outside Stockholm.*

even more appealing, and the prospect of owning a summer residence on lakeside or seashore became increasingly desirable especially for the increasing number of urban dwellers.

By the mid-1800s enterprising builders had begun to erect houses for sale or rent on leased or freehold plots. Panelled wooden cottages with verandas on two or more floors and stairwells in the form of towers were the norm. The projecting roofs and elaborate fret-saw ornamentation, called 'gingerbread work', on the eaves, bargeboards and verandas were typical features of what was known at the time as the 'Alpine', 'Swiss Cottage' or 'chalet' style of building. One major influence on this style was the series of engravings published by the architect Charles Emil Löfvenskiöld, the first of which, *Landtmannabyggnader* (rural buildings) by C. A. Forselius, appeared in 1854-5. Forselius's illustrations showed the timbered frames of houses covered with a decorative network of ornamentation, panels and contour-sawn doorframes and window reveals.

As the century progressed, the *nouveaux riches* wholesalers and factory owners competed in their endeavours to outdo one another by building increasingly imaginative summer houses on hitherto unexploited islands in the skerries. Summer pavilions, towers and belvederes affording spectacular views of the surrounding scenery appeared on top of rocky outcrops, while down by the water's edge boathouses rubbed shoulders with bathing huts, and guest houses and hotels were built at each of the steamers' ports of call.

As the nineteenth century drew to a close the distinction between summer homes and permanent dwellings became less apparent: often it was only the location of the house – close to open water – that revealed its function as a summer home. The summer houses in the skerries were now being built with two storeys, and the shallow roofs so much admired at the beginning of the century had given way to steep, high ones, covered in roofing felt, sheet metal or red tiles. The exteriors of these homes were adorned by ornate

verandas, and sometimes by spires and cupolas. The wood panelling of the façades was usually painted either red, yellow or white, but green and blue painted boards could also be seen, as well as shiny black shingle cladding. Green, blue and red panes of glass, often lozenge-shaped in the mullioned windows, contributed to this rich kaleidoscope of colour – especially on the verandas.

The kind of lifestyle embraced by 'simple' people who subsisted on agriculture, fishing and apiary had been idealized by the influential writer Carl Jonas Love Almqvist in the first half of the nineteenth century. 'Returning' to this bucolic idyll became a dream nurtured by the urban classes who, as the century wore on, were gradually encouraged to try to realize this dream – at least during the summer months.

The natural spring at Medevi in Östergötland was first popularized in the late 1600s under the royal patronage of Queen Hedvig Eleonora. Seventy or so timber buildings, painted or rendered on the outside, soon sprang up around the baths and church, and by the time Queen Ulrika Eleonora the Younger and King Fredrik I visited the spa in the eighteenth century to seek a cure for their infertility, the spa had been transformed into a village in its own right.

FAR LEFT *The so-called Doctor's House at Medevi was decorated in the 1790s with distemper on paper sheets glued to the timber walls. The table and chair are typical of the simple furniture of summer houses in the eighteenth century; originally table and chair would either have been painted a darker colour, such as blue-grey, or stained to resemble mahogany; early this century they were painted white with the details picked out in bronze.*

CENTRE *The only stone building at Medevi, apart from the chapel, the Pump Room was built in the first half of the nineteenth century in Neo-Classical style, but with Neo-Gothic touches in the tracery of the fanlights. Taking the waters, which were ladled out to visitors here in the Pump Room, was the focal point of Medevi's informal yet strictly regimented social life.*

LEFT *The main dining hall in the refectory at Medevi was built in the mid-eighteenth century. The wall decorations, however, were heavily restored on at least two or three occasions during the first half of the nineteenth century. The walls of vertical boards, faux marble dado and overdoor are from the 1750s, whereas the painted pilasters and the ceiling frieze date from the early 1800s.*

If owning one's own summer house was out of the question for reasons of expense, one alternative was to hire rooms from the locals. This was favoured by people such as the author August Strindberg, and other cultural celebrities at the end of the 1800s.

Increasing prosperity during this century, and especially after the Second World War, has enabled many more people to buy houses as summer retreats. First and foremost it was the Stockholm archipelago which attracted summer visitors, or the Swedish west coast where the water was less brackish. Small west-coast towns such as Båstad, Varberg and Marstrand came alive during the summer months and now some of the old fishing villages have been transformed into summer resorts for town dwellers.

Sund

PREVIOUS PAGES *The timber-framed manor house of Sund was clad with boards and endowed with lavishly decorated window surrounds, bargeboards and verandas in the second half of the nineteenth century.*

The glazed veranda projecting from the front façade leads into a succession of reception rooms. In keeping with early twentieth-century eclecticism, the decoration here encompasses a variety of styles. The furniture inclines towards Gustavian and late Empire ideals: the white tiled stove, typical of the kind produced around 1800, exhibits Classical features in the shape of its columnar chimney and rectangular base, but is nevertheless embellished with distinctly Neo-Rococo flourishes. The plain white ceiling and untreated wooden floorboards add an even greater emphasis to the eighteenth-century character of the room that is so ably conjured up by the furnishings: the gilt mirror, the Gustavian chest-of-drawers inlaid with various woods, the light grey Gustavian chairs with their checked upholstery, and the simple white curtains.

The Gustavian footstools grouped around the circular folding table date from a slightly later, Empire, period, while the plethora of large potted plants is a vestige of the taste of the late nineteenth and early twentieth century when the atmosphere of the conservatory, a fashion introduced from England in about the mid-1800s, was much sought after.

Although it is now used as a summer house, Sund began life as a manor house set amid the trees and arable lands of the island of Värmdö in the Stockholm archipelago. It acquired a new owner in the 1870s when it was rebuilt with elaborate 'gingerbread work' on its façade, and is still owned by descendants of the family.

With the exception of the dining room – which is decorated in the heavy Renaissance style that was the most fashionable decor for dining rooms during the last years of the nineteenth century – the interiors owe much to the Arts and Crafts Movement and to Carl Larsson's home at Sundborn. These twin influences are apparent in the translucent white linen curtains that replace the heavy swathes of late-nineteenth-century drapery, and in the lighter, less cluttered style that pervades Sund even though it was rebuilt and furnished during a period when more elaborate and contrived design was in vogue.

LEFT *This ground-floor veranda forms a prominent projecting bay on the front façade. Light filters in through the large windows dressed with white muslin blinds hanging from white-painted metal poles and through the pierced walls that give the veranda an exotic character. The other walls and the ceiling are clad with tongue-and-groove boards. The informality of a rural existence is reflected in the furnishing: a pot-pourri of Gustavian upholstered seats (painted white and gold at some point in the nineteenth century), an Art Nouveau-style table and simple, rustic stick-back chairs. The wide window sills provide plenty of space for the potted plants that are so treasured for their summer colours.*

FAR LEFT *Family keepsakes in the form of portraits, paintings and embroidered pictures hang in strict symmetry above a rustic late-Empire sofa. The stylized Art Nouveau flowers on the wallpaper continue the mid-nineteenth-century tradition of covering walls with textile imitations.*

Tegelön

ABOVE *Originally built as a pavilion and regularly used for private dances and festivities during the early twentieth century, this building on the island of Tegelön is now the home of the artist Sigvard Olsson. The verandas, which were originally open to the elements, were glazed in the 1930s.*

RIGHT *The Olsson summer home exhibits a charming pot-pourri of furnishings and fittings in different styles from different times. A flamboyant Neo-Rococo chaise longue from the middle of the nineteenth century is balanced by a rustic Gustavian stool from the eighteenth century; both mix easily with white lacquered Art Nouveau-style chairs.*

LEFT *The combination of the tall, angular late Gustavian stove with its Pompeian ornamentation in subdued sepia tones, and the tower-like staircase leading to a gable room under the raftered ceiling bestows a rare artistic harmony on the large salon in the Olsson home. This is enhanced by the slenderness of the tall double doors, the serenity of the monochrome walls, and the simplicity of the painted floor and furniture. It is a lesson in the art of restraint.*

The stove was rescued from a Stockholm house due for demolition and was installed here by the Olssons. Stoves in Classical garb first appeared in the 1780s, but some twenty years were to pass before they achieved any real popularity. By 1810 monochrome tiled stoves had all but superseded the polychromatic ones and became the very pinnacle of fashion. As repeated motifs began to lose ground to architecturally painted stoves in the 1790s, friezes and central motifs became increasingly common. Around the same time, unglazed ceramic plinths, painted to imitate porphyry or marble, began to replace the wooden or iron legs which previously served as bases for the stoves.

As the nineteenth century drew to a close, a number of substantial houses were built on the island of Tegelön in the Stockholm archipelago. Like most summer homes, they were decorated with verandas, often two-storey affairs offering panoramic vistas out over the water. Either glazed or left open to the elements, these are often referred to as 'punch verandas', in veneration of the contemporary fashion for drinking Swedish arrack punch while entertaining guests in the afternoons or long summer evenings. Glazed verandas together with large windows helped to create both close contact with the natural world outside and a cosy atmosphere indoors.

RIGHT *The glazed veranda of the artist's home that overlooks a quiet stretch of water displays the simplicity associated with the concept of the Swedish summer house. The unabashed arrangement of a disparate collection of early-twentieth-century chairs round the eighteenth-century white-painted drop-leaf table shows how the modern furnishing ideal tends to be functional and utilitarian rather than slavishly pure in style.*

ABOVE AND LEFT *This late-nineteenth-century house on the island of Tegelön only a stone's throw from the water's edge illustrates the delightful, typical location of these summer homes. The addition of open and glazed verandas, lavishly decorated window surrounds and pierced woodwork lend the unmistakable aura of the Swedish summer home to what would otherwise be merely a traditional red-painted wooden house. Inside the glazed veranda what were once outside walls have now been painted yellow.*

The nostalgic longing for a rustic folk culture that was first recognized in Carl Larsson's days over a century ago, is still a strong decorative force. The owners of this house have sought to evoke the flavour of the past in imaginative new ways, as witnessed here by the simple chairs painted blue and white, and the drop leaf table used in combination with the ornate late-nineteenth-century oil lamp. At the same time, they have endeavoured to make their home as practical and easy to care for as possible by using, for example, sealed floors in place of what would have been old scrubbed deal boards.

The yearning for a life in an unexploited environment close to nature was one of the driving forces behind the exodus of many people to the tranquillity of depopulated areas such as the island of Gotland which lies between the Swedish mainland and the Baltic states. Local building materials, such as limestone and mortar from the island's own lime-kilns, have given Gotland's traditional vernacular architecture a style all of its own, although timber or half-timbered houses exist alongside the more typical white-rendered limestone houses.

Influences from the mainland, though slow to percolate as far as Gotland, can also be seen in some of the grander houses: in the seventeenth-century two-storeyed farmhouses that were built bearing a resemblance to the manor houses of the mainland from the first half of that century; and in the rendered brickwork and pitched roofs of the eighteenth-century mansions of the Gotland nobility that look to the Rococo architecture of Stockholm. However, the poorer smallholders and fishermen's families continued to use time-hallowed building methods, constructing massive limestone walls and thatching the high roofs with reeds or seaweed as their prehistoric ancestors had.

It is these smaller homes on the coast that hold the greatest attraction for the twentieth-century seekers of simplicity and cultural heritage. Many buildings were 'modernized' in the late nineteenth century with industrially produced printed wallpaper, but the new owners have tended to follow in the footsteps of local museums and have removed these wallcoverings, either revealing and restoring the original colours and decorations, or simply painting the walls white. Antique shops and farmyard auctions have provided one obvious furnishing route but contemporary designs such as bentwood or chrome-plated tubular steel furniture have also been used with aesthetic success.

Overall, however, a lack of conventional status symbols in decoration and furnishings continues to be a characteristic of Swedish summer houses. Of far greater importance than socially prestigious interiors are the natural surroundings and the chance to live a freer, less sophisticated life during the short summer.

ABOVE *The island of Gotland is, for the most part, rather flat, and the towering spires of the churches, which punctuate the sky like so many raised spears, are often visible for miles.*

OPPOSITE TOP *Renovated by the glass artist Rolf Sinnemark, this stone house was originally a brewhouse. The lack of bargeboards and the abrupt termination of the roofing tiles, which do not extend over the gables, are typical characteristics of the houses on Gotland, and lend such properties an almost Mediterranean, 'Cubist' quality.*

OPPOSITE CENTRE *The eighteenth-century fashion from mainland Sweden for symmetrical, six-roomed houses has left its mark on Gotland's architectural landscape in the ground plans of many of the island's wooden cottages and stone farmhouses. One of these six-roomed houses, at Urgarde, is now the home of textile artist Brita Wassdahl.*

OPPOSITE BELOW *Their roofs covered with rough wooden tiles, these Lilliputian cottages that once sheltered fishermen are now summer houses for visitors from the mainland.*

Groddegården

ABOVE *The fortress-like appearance of Groddegården Farm, on the road to Fårösund in the north of Gotland, makes the house look considerably older than it is. The lower floor was built in the seventeenth century or perhaps slightly earlier, but the upper one was not added until the middle of the following century. The structure of the house shows, however, that building techniques had changed little since the island's golden age in the thirteenth and fourteenth centuries.*

LEFT *This ground-floor room boasts an open fireplace incorporating limestone relics of an earlier Renaissance surround in its faux marble chimneypiece. The chimneypiece acquired its current appearance around the middle of the last century, at the same time as the walls and cornice were stencilled. This type of painted wall decoration soon became a popular substitute for more expensive, early-nineteenth-century printed wallpapers and paper friezes.*

ABOVE *What began as one of the main rooms on the upper floor was divided into two smaller rooms, probably around the middle of the nineteenth century when it was wallpapered. This wallpaper was removed during the most recent renovation of the house and, using traces of the original paint as a guide, the walls were repainted. The grey dado that extends from the floor to the height of the window sill is a feature that was typical of many interiors all over Sweden from the end of the 1700s until the advent of factory-printed rolls of wallpaper in the 1860s. The extendable bed is of a type that would have been standard for reasonably well-off families, such as those who lived at Groddegården between 1870 and 1900. 'Imperial' beds like this one tended to be painted either pale grey (see page 172) or dark reddish-brown to resemble mahogany, as in this example.*

Groddegården, which takes its name from the famous Groddes folk musician family, once served as an inn. It is now a local museum, run by a group of enthusiasts who have recently renovated the rooms using authentic techniques to reproduce the old colours and patterns. The rooms are furnished with pieces made in Gotland, where carpenters and joiners tended to simplify the forms and features seen on the mainland. This is particularly noticeable in the chairs, in which the lines of continental Baroque designs have been simplified and their woven cane backs and seats replaced with wooden rails and seats. In this part of the country old-fashioned techniques and traditional design in woodwork lingered longer than elsewhere. The ornate single-panelled door provides a good illustration of this phenomenon: the same design can be seen on cupboard doors and doors to the box-pews installed in many of Sweden's churches during the 1600s.

RIGHT *Some of the dividing walls on the upper floor at Groddegården consist merely of vertical boards. In one of the rooms off the landing is an open fireplace in the Baroque style of around 1700. This is an example of the kind of ornamental masonry which was produced on Gotland during the seventeenth and eighteenth centuries for the manor houses then being built both in Stockholm and throughout central Sweden. The fireplace surround was probably originally made with the intention of shipping it to the mainland, but, for some reason or other, it never left the island and was later installed and used during Groddegården's years as an inn.*

Itinerant painters in Dalarna, Hälsingland and Gästrikland

THE

RURAL

TRADITION

Even though they lie far south of the country's geographical centre, the provinces of Dalarna, Hälsingland and Gästrikland are referred to in Sweden as Norrland, 'the Northlands'. These three provinces, which stretch in a broad swathe across Sweden from the borders of Norway to the shores of the Baltic Sea, are the fount of a rural peasant culture that has bequeathed a rich legacy of vernacular art. Based very broadly on the forms of architecture and interior decoration espoused by the upper classes who lived in or near Stockholm, this art developed its own formula of an extraordinary vivacity and strength which has come to be much valued and emulated in the twentieth century.

The wealth that enabled the tradition to flourish was founded on the provinces' natural resources of iron, copper, timber and flax. Iron was produced from limonite or bog iron during the Middle Ages, after which the emphasis shifted to mining. Production increased and was to be of enormous signficance for Sweden's export trade from the seventeenth to the nineteenth centuries. Copper was also important and was extracted from the rich veins at Falun in Dalarna, which also gave its name to the distinctive red iron oxide paint that was produced there.

The export of timber and woven linen began in the 1600s: planks from Hälsingland, for example, were shipped to Stockholm to be used as floors and ceilings in the city's new stone houses. Trade was stepped up after the Peace of Nystad in 1721, as part of the movement to revitalize the Swedish economy after the crippling effects of a twenty-year war. The state also invested heavily in the production of, among other things, damask in the little parish of Flor in Hälsingland. It was here that the finest damask cloths and napkins in Sweden were woven to meet the needs of the royal household.

The sale of minerals, timber and linen was the chief reason why, by the nineteenth century, the peasant classes in this part of the country had the financial resources to create such well-built timber farmhouses, the largest in Sweden. Neither common sense nor practical advantage dictated the size of these wooden buildings – sometimes several crowded round just a single farmyard. They were designed, rather, as an overt display of wealth, and also as the provinces' answer to the manor houses built for Stockholm's aristocracy during the second half of the eighteenth century.

Until the end of the eighteenth century single-storey houses remained the norm even among the wealthiest of farmers, but then two- and sometimes even three-storey homes began to appear. Adding an extra floor to older houses was not as expensive as it might appear: the wealth tax that was current between 1790 and 1809 was not payable on unused rooms, so the upper floors of many of the larger homes were left undecorated – and in many instances have remained so ever

PREVIOUS PAGES *The decoration above the entrance to a Hälsingland cottage that was built in the 1830s is a vernacular version of Gustavian stone portals of the 1780s and 1790s.*
LEFT *The wooden walls, ceiling and door of the 'best room' in Andurstugan at Bortomåa on the borders of Dalarna and Hälsingland were painted by an itinerant local artist as part of the preparations for a wedding on the farm in the summer of 1821.*
ABOVE *This naive* trompe l'oeil *frame enclosing a stylized landscape and an abundant horn of plenty was painted in 1790 and comes from Pålsgården in Gästrikland.*

143

ABOVE LEFT *The shape of the wrought-iron handle on a door at Kristoffer Stensgården in Hälsingland has remained unchanged since medieval times.*

ABOVE RIGHT *This turned wooden door handle from Delsbogården, now at Skansen open-air museum, dates from the early years of the nineteenth century.*

RIGHT *Visitors to Masmästaregården are welcomed by the spreading boughs of Trees of Life painted directly onto the boarded walls. This old house, which was renovated in c.1790 and extended with the addition of an upper floor, was built in Gästrikland but is now part of the local museum at Järbo. Interest in the Tree of Life motif enjoyed a revival during the late 1700s when Sweden was swept by a fascination for botany popularized by engravings of exotic flowers. Masmästaregården was occupied by a bergsman, a superintendent of the local mines, who was also a masmästare or owner of the blast-furnace in which iron ore was smelted. Thanks to his elevated position and the relative prosperity which accompanied it, the house was decorated at an earlier date than most of the others in Gästrikland. In this hallway there are suggestions of a Renaissance-style Tree of Life in the large-scale decorative scheme, adapted from the limewashed walls of the churches and the royal palaces. In the room beyond are more Trees of Life, this time in pots, painted some time towards the end of the eighteenth century.*

since. Some of the farms of Hälsingland which truly deserve the epithet 'wooden palaces' boast over 250 square metres (3,000 square feet) of living space; of this, perhaps only half at the most was ever in use.

The exteriors of these houses were usually unpainted until the middle of the nineteenth century, after which the rusty glow of Falu red paint gradually became more common. At the same time, the planks or shingles that had been used for roofs were superseded by red-brown roofing tiles, and projecting porches – usually painted in a contrasting colour – were added, giving a new significance to the front door.

It is possible to identify certain similarities between the ground plans of the cottages of the seventeenth and eighteenth centuries of the farmer-miners in southern Dalarna and Gästrikland and those of the farmhouses in Hälsingland built during the following century. Most of the early single-storey wooden cottages were built on the so-called *parstuga* principle. Literally the *parstuga* is a 'double cottage' consisting of two adjacent but distinct sections, linked and separated by an entrance hall. On one side of this hall was the main living room, leading to a second room beyond, on the other side was a 'best room', sometimes also referred to as the

The 'best room' on the ground floor of Delsbogården is now part of the open-air museum at Skansen in Stockholm. Built originally in Hälsingland, the house was decorated in 1819 by two painters, the brothers Erik and Anders Andersson from Leksand in Dalarna. The prevalence of red and blue is a typical feature of Leksand's artistic traditions. Even though the painters frequently drew their inspiration from the Bible, the dramatis personae *were invariably dressed in the most fashionable of contemporary clothes. The furniture, pushed up close to the walls, reflects the interior decorating style of the salons of the eighteenth-century manor houses: there is the customary drop-leaf table and a suite of chairs (albeit with black-painted wooden seats in place of the leather-upholstered ones which one would expect to find in the manors). The sill-height dado is spatter-painted on a grey background. Rooms like this would often sport a boldly painted cornice, to make a clear border between the busy walls and the plain whitewashed ceiling.*

The Rural Tradition

OPPOSITE *Porches provided shelter from snow and rain, and were also a popular place to sit during the summer. Like the design of the doors, they were also an opportunity for self-expression. This temple-like portico dated 1853, in Hälsingland, dignifies an ordinary home with an entrance fit for a public building (ABOVE NEAR RIGHT). Stylized Classical features are enhanced by the fluted, decorative panels of the double door of a house in Hälsingland (ABOVE CENTRE). Monumentality has been softened with a gently curved pediment at Olandersgården in Hälsingland (ABOVE FAR RIGHT). Curved supports are enlivened by the profiled bargeboards and by the painted pediment, dated 1842, at Olasgården, in Hälsingland (BELOW NEAR RIGHT). Contour-sawn Rococo curves decorate the early nineteenth-century porch at Karlsgården in Hälsingland (BELOW CENTRE). Although this cottage in Dalarna is new, the combination of unpainted wood with the red and blue doorframes and bargeboards is deeply rooted in local tradition (BELOW FAR RIGHT).*

BELOW *Contrary to popular belief, the two-storey, red-painted Swedish farmhouse only became common some years into the nineteenth century. Before that, most rural homes were unpainted single-storey constructions, although an upper storey was often added as soon as the economy of the farm permitted. This farmhouse is now a museum. It is obvious from the non-aligned windows and from the boxed-in end timbers of the original entrance hall walls – visible on either side of the porch – that an upper floor and porch have been added.*

LEFT *The decoration in this guest room of a house from Sunnanås in Hälsingland is a mix of Gustavian delicacy and local tradition. The walls, papered and coated with thick limewash, were probably decorated by an itinerant painter.*

ABOVE *This window belongs to a guest cottage attached to the house dating from about 1830. Behind the glazing bars the roller blind, in reality, fills the window but is painted to give the illusion that it is resting above a window sill of flowerpots.*

RIGHT *In the main Sunnanås house a wall is stencilled in a lacy pattern inspired by contemporary French wallpapers, while beneath the dado rail it is spattered in grey, black and white to look like granite. Painting directly onto timber has a long history in Sweden; wallpaper was expensive and in short supply whereas colour pigments, chalk and glue were cheap and plentiful.*

'feast room'. The farming communities of Gästrikland and Hälsingland adopted the ground plan of the *parstuga*, adding extra floors or building extensions and annexes.

The houses were, to a greater or lesser degree, decorated by itinerant decorative painters, most of them hailing from Dalarna. These roving artists chose their motifs from two sources. One was religious: the oldest forms of wall and ceiling decoration in the farmhouses of the region probably stem from the painted vaults and ceilings of the churches. These church paintings date from the late Middle Ages and the

Renaissance, and their motifs are taken directly from the stories of the Bible, or possibly copied from some of the hundreds of woodcuts used to illustrate the Gustav II Adolf Bible, which was printed in Stockholm in 1619. As a selection of these woodcuts also appeared in other religious works, they were easily the most accessible models for the itinerant artists, and remained so right up until the nineteenth century.

The church painters were often the same men who would decorate the cottages, so there is a natural explanation for the

ABOVE *Gustavian features, such as fluting, stylized leaves and mouldings appear on the front doors of a nineteenth-century farm in Hälsingland.*

LEFT *Kristoffer Stensgården in Hälsingland was decorated in the mid-nineteenth century. The stencilled walls use a pattern that is a provincial simplification of Empire-style printed wallpapers. In the room beyond, however, the painted motifs look back to the eighteenth century.*

OPPOSITE *As in so many homes which have remained in continuous use, the nineteenth-century decoration of Per Larsgården in Hälsingland is now hidden. But the bedroom boasts its original 'cupboard bed' – the footboard forms a closet – whose doors are typical of the richly painted furniture of the rural peasants.*

close links between the *faux* marbling and graining of the pews, pulpits and retables in the churches and the decorative techniques used in the homes of the farmers and miners.

The second source of inspiration for the local artists was secular: the interior schemes of manor houses were adapted and interpreted according to local skills, and then these adaptions were reinterpreted. Painted imitations of Gobelin wallhangings executed on coarse linen fabric that were such a characteristic feature of the Baroque manors appear, for example, in a different guise in the home of Carolus Linnaeus's in-laws at Sveden, east of Falun. An annexe there, built in the 1700s, is decorated with linen canvas painted to mimic Gobelin tapestries with motifs taken from the Old Testament story of King David. (This annexe is known as the 'Wedding House' because, on 26 June 1739, it was the setting for Linnaeus's marriage, and it is possible that it was built specifically to celebrate this event.)

LEFT AND BELOW *In 1934 the local history society at Norrala in Hälsingland acquired this two-storey house that dates from 1846. Despite its mid-nineteenth-century origins, it preserves exactly the traditions of eighteenth-century building techniques in its floors, boarded dadoes and the profiled window frames and architraves. It is only the painted paper and canvas on the walls that disclose its real age. The finest rooms on both the ground and upper floors have been decorated with stencilled patterns. On the upper floor, stencils imitate the vertical patterns of printed wallpapers: curling blue tendrils form the borders for the central floral motifs. The cornice was almost certainly originally decorated with similar stencilled designs, or perhaps even a paper border, but this has since been lost. In the ground-floor parlour, stencilled patterns form decorative corners for a series of landscapes. As in many local museums, the furniture is not an accurate reflection of the home's original inventory, but rather a motley accumulation of appropriate items from a number of sources.*

As the eighteenth century drew to a close, increased contacts with the fashionable interiors of the manor houses and the mansions in the towns encouraged decorative painters in Gästrikland and Hälsingland as well as in Dalarna to try their hand at imitating secular models. Festoons of painted flowers, sometimes in *faux* panelling frames, reveal the influence of Gustavian Classicism, which by now was also beginning to enjoy some popularity in the provincial towns. Other much-favoured painted motifs include urns brimming with flowers, and the 'Tree of Life' which came in a wide range of guises borrowed, almost certainly, from botanical treatises or from the woodcut vignettes of religious tracts. Next to the Gustav II Adolf Bible the most widely used model for decorative painters in the provinces was probably *Suecia Antiqua et Hodierna*, a series of copperplate engravings of palaces, manor houses, churches and towns. From the 1830s onwards, motifs of townscapes and landscapes dotted with buildings began to appear more frequently, probably due to

the increasing influence of the pictorial wallpapers imported from France.

In kitchens, vestibules and other less elaborately decorated rooms, stencilled patterns or spatter painting were the most common techniques used. Spatter painting to feign the appearance of granite was usually reserved for the dado and rarely extended above the sill of the windows.

As the century wore on, the commercial value of timber began to be seriously exploited: sawmill owners and merchants moved in, procuring concessions and rights to the forests, and buying out smallholdings. This began a process of attrition of local skills and traditions, exacerbated by land reforms which broke up village communities. For a short period, as a sort of swansong, houses were built and decorated with greater exuberance than before. The manufacture of industrially produced items, such as doors, windows, wallpaper, stoves and furniture, further and eventually fatally impoverished a once-rich peasant culture.

Rural painting traditions experienced a revival towards the middle of the nineteenth century although the motifs still looked to the past, to as much as fifty years or even a century before.

LEFT *A room decorated during the second half of the nineteenth century has been preserved in its original condition in what is now the home of the keen local historian, Ulla Hanser, in the parish of Alfta in Hälsingland. Above the brown-painted dado, the boarded walls are painted as an arcade complete with Ionic columns, exotic trees and shrubs against a lively sky in various shades of blue. The columns are entwined with climbing vines and the arches decorated with leafy green designs. The verve and infectious enthusiasm of the painter overrides the undeniable naivety of the result to conjure up a mood suggesting a dreamworld or some exotic foreign landscape.*

RIGHT *The walls of this house in Fågelsjö in Dalarna were painted in about 1850 on paper glued directly to the timber walls. The central 'picture' with its stylized drapery that recalls the window dressing of the Empire period, is meant to look like a view through a window – with a vase of flowers presumably sitting on the sill.*
The grey dado is spattered with white and black paint to resemble granite, and the furniture is stippled to feign wood with a more interesting grain such as walnut.

THE PAST AS

INSPIRATION

Restoring and recreating
period homes

To understand why so many Swedes aspire to own an old house with antique furnishings, or seek to emulate the decorating styles of the past, one needs to be aware of the changes in lifestyle and the developments in attitude that have taken place over the past century and a half. It is fascinating to see how increasing industrialization and the gradual disintegration of an age-old way of life have been accompanied by a growing awareness of not only the values associated with the past, but also of Sweden's architectural heritage. Until the middle of the nineteenth century Sweden was largely an agrarian society, and home-building and interior decoration developed only within the limits of local traditions; but after that, advances in technology using innovations such as steam power began to have an increasing effect on social structures and consequently on architecture and interiors.

Following the introduction of new processes elsewhere in Europe, the old ironworks – which had been the centre of close-knit patriarchal communities – suddenly found themselves forced to close as large-scale production moved to a few major centres. Meanwhile, factories were taking over the production of many of the goods that had previously been made at home, and the country's rail network expanded to meet the transport needs of the growing timber industry.

Agriculture, too, was rapidly changing. Increasing demand for exports to the continent, especially of cereal, resulted in the reorganization of the traditional system of scattered strips of pasture, field and forest into larger, enclosed holdings which produced better yields. This had far-reaching consequences. Old village communities were split up; land-owning farmers built new homes adjacent to the compact areas of land allotted to them, while the peasant farmers and smallholders on large estates gradually found themselves working as agricultural labourers, housed in tied cottages where they no longer enjoyed security of tenure.

The sum of all these changes was to have a disastrous effect on rural culture. Fortunately, a few people had the vision to realize what was happening, and *Svenska slöjdföreningen*, a sort of Swedish handicrafts association, was founded in the 1840s to collect samples of arts and crafts to serve as a source of inspiration for manufacturers. In 1872, King Carl XV donated his own eclectic collections to the state in an attempt to institute some form of Museum of Arts and Crafts (in the event this was first established at the royal palace of Ulriksdal, north of Stockholm, a hundred years later). The King had a particular fondness for the Renaissance and Baroque periods and furnished his private apartments not only with magnificent antiques but also with specially commissioned new pieces in the relevant style. Having reproduction furniture made based on historical precedents in order to create complete period interiors was something that was soon adopted by private individuals.

PREVIOUS PAGES *Flaming cannonballs at Länna Manor are fitting ornaments for a house built in the mid-seventeenth century for an ironworks proprietor.*
LEFT *The concept of using old furniture in new ways derives, to a great extent, from the impact made by Carl and Karin Larsson's home at Sundborn. The eighteenth-century stove in Karin's bedroom lacks both its original base and shallower top section, but for the Larssons, the stove's hand-painted floral decoration was more important than any strict historical accuracy in either appearance or installation. The same disregard is seen in the repainted blue nightstand and decoration around the door. The detail (ABOVE) is from a frieze painted by their daughter in much the same style as her father's.*

OPPOSITE NEAR RIGHT *Carl Larsson's watercolour of the parlour at Sundborn in the mid 1890s.*
No other home has had quite such an influence on Swedish interior decoration over the past hundred years as that
of the artist Carl Larsson and his wife Karin at Lilla Hyttnäs in Sundborn, and it is perhaps images of this room,
more than any other, that have rekindled interest in the timeless qualities of historical interiors. The mélange of
the restrained elegance of the eighteenth century seen in a Rococo chair and the faux panels and cast-brass
candelabra on the wall, with white-painted early nineteenth-century pieces was refreshingly liberated from the
constrictions of contemporary interior decoration. In the late 1800s, collectors' homes were usually cluttered with
valuable rarities from the eighteenth-century ébénistes, and the doors and windows were swathed in complex
curtaining arrangements. Perhaps Sundborn's most significant contribution to interior decorating style was the
reintroduction of scrubbed wooden floors as an acceptable alternative to the fitted carpets, parquet and parquet-
patterned linoleum which, by the 1890s, were being laid indiscriminately.

LEFT *The extraordinary mixture of styles in the dining room at Sundborn is held together by Carl Larsson's idiosyncratic interpretation of each.*
The decoration on the plastered wall could well be a manifesto for the Larssons' Weltanschauung. *Superimposed on a cartouche of the French Revolution's 'Liberté, Egalité, Fraternité' – the rallying call which once again became topical during Carl Larsson's years as a young artist in France in the 1870s – is a banner proclaiming the motto 'Love one another, my Children, for Love is Everything.' A door blocked off during one of the house's numerous renovations has been redesigned as a buffet, with a folding, semi-circular serving table – one of the many eye-catching innovations that have inspired a number of imitators. Like so many other artists and cultural celebrities of the time, the Larssons were subscribers to the influential English journal* The Studio. *The inspiration for the quatrefoil quattrocento motifs on the upper doors came from the English Arts and Crafts Movement. The dining chairs (provincial translations of*

Gustavian originals), and the skirtings and display shelf have been painted red, making a strong colour contrast to the green of the tongue-and-groove half-wainscoted walls. It was this type of arrangement that helped to revive the fashion for symmetry.

ABOVE RIGHT *The fact that this window could be described as an innovation, a pastiche or a refinement of an old Swedish tradition, reveals something of the universality of the decoration at Sundborn. While the idea of the framed panel below the window clearly owes much to Gustavian Classicism, the painting itself is a mixture of Dutch seventeenth-century motifs and French nineteenth-century Romanticism. The white muslin curtain is hung using narrow bands of fabric instead of rings; the design of the acorn finials on the pole is almost certainly one of Carl Larsson's.*

The enthusiasm of the King for past styles also stimulated the restoration of royal residences including that of Gripsholm Castle. Despite some criticism directed at the restorers' occasionally heavy-handed approach, popular interest in the past – bolstered by the contemporary fixation for the great figures of Swedish history – was aroused.

Arthur Hazelius created the Nordic Museum and the open-air museum at Skansen in Stockholm towards the end of the century, thereby igniting an idea that has become an important element of Swedish cultural life, namely the establishment of a repository of the past, and a sanctuary for homes and interiors that would otherwise be demolished. By the turn of the century local folklore societies were being formed throughout the country. Dedicated to the preservation of local buildings and the promotion of arts and crafts, they set up the *hembygdsgård*, a place where older, unoccupied houses and interiors could be rebuilt and studied.

During the 1920s Skogaholm, a typical eighteenth-century manor house, was moved and rebuilt at Skansen. Although conceived as a representation of the domestic life of Sweden's upper classes, it has since become a source of inspiration for the many people who have sought to decorate their homes in

Hans Keijser, an architect, and his wife, Kerstin, redecorated a wing of the eighteenth-century manor at Ekensberg using a mix of historical styles. They have chosen to leave the whitewashed ceilings as they were, but have painted many of the doorframes and window frames with different colours.

NEAR RIGHT *The bedroom is dominated by a large four-poster bed, and home-woven rag rugs lie on the bare floorboards. The walls have been spatter-painted using colours and techniques that look to those of the late eighteenth century.*

FAR RIGHT *The built-in beds hidden behind curtains, based on rural alcove beds, are new to the house. The simple chair in the foreground and the grey drop-leaf table are original, whereas the wooden chandelier is a copy made with the aid of books on old Swedish joinery techniques.*

eighteenth-century fashion. Initially, interest in this period had been restricted to collectors, who concentrated chiefly on endeavouring to recreate the more magnificent interior styles of the time. What was new in the way the manor-house ideal was interpreted at Skansen was the modesty and lack of pretension of its checked and striped seat covers, printed cotton textiles and bare wooden floors. The interior decoration of the two annexes in particular, one reconstructed as a kitchen pavilion, the other as combined library and guest apartments, shows that, in many essentials, everyday life for the inhabitants of the manor houses differed little from that of those in the farmhouses.

It is the synthesis of the elegant and the utilitarian that remains so appealing – the hand-painted wall decoration, the glazed tiled stoves and the uncluttered appearance of the rooms. This is the quintessence of the Swedish manor house, with its painted surfaces and furniture, scrubbed deal floors, diaphanous curtaining and rooms flooded with natural light. It is the heritage that Carl Larsson emulated in his house in Sundborn, and that he so ably communicated through his paintings. It is a legacy that continues to exert the same fascination for us today.

Rather than endeavouring to recapture the original character of the house – which was built in the early 1800s as a sergeant's quarters – or attempting to re-create a particular historical era or environment, Lars Olsson has chosen to use it as a setting for his eclectic collection of furniture and objets d'art.
A late-Gustavian mahogany table, its top inset with a kaleidoscope of polished stones, stands on a hand-knotted Oriental rug in the centre of the 'best room'. Hanging above is a bronze lantern from the 1780s or 1790s. The grey-painted bookcase adorned with beribboned laurel wreaths and festoons is made of pine, after Jean Eric Rehn's designs for libraries and scientific collections. The seat covers are a testament to Olsson's aversion to the bland pastiches that masquerade as 'period fabrics'; instead he uses leather and hard-wearing new fabrics in bright monochrome colours.

Länna Gård

ABOVE *Built in the 1650s and modernized a century later, Länna is a Swedish wooden version of a Palladian villa. Its two-storey main building has a Mansard roof, the upper slope covered with metal plate, the lower with tiles, and the façades are clad in yellow-painted boards.*

LEFT *The original simple ground plan of the house has been preserved: the view here looks from an anteroom at one end of the house, across the entrance hall, to the kitchen at the other end. The architectural shell has also remained remarkably intact – the plain board ceiling, the cornice, the panelled wooden dado and the tall double doors all belong to the 1770s. The stove, with its vigorous pattern of blue leaves and its painted wooden feet, although not original to the house, is of the same date. The walls above the dado are a strikingly successful mélange of styles. The shape and size of the recently painted wall panels are inspired by mid-eighteenth-century wall decorations.*

The manor house of Länna, in Uppland, was built for Baron Claes Rålamb, Marshal of the Realm in the mid-seventeenth century, and proprietor of a nearby ironworks. Although it has changed hands many times during the last three hundred years, its current owners, Jan and Ingrid Holmberg, have worked with devotion and determination to restore its true historical character.

RIGHT *The delightful rustic elegance of the kitchen at Länna, both in the individual furnishings and accessories, and in the way in which they have been combined, belies the fact that this is also a practical, modern kitchen.*

Reproduction plate shelves, filled chiefly with old East Indies porcelain on the left, and with blue and sepia Swedish faience from Rörstrand and Marieberg on the right, lend a strong symmetry to the wall of the kitchen – a symmetry that is emphasized by the twin Rococo buffets. The table is surrounded by rustic ladderback chairs that have the Baroque lines that remained popular in the provinces until the end of the 1700s. There are strong echoes here, in the colours, crockery and furniture, of the porcelain kitchen at Thureholm, which has become one of the most widely admired interiors in Sweden.

The large eighteenth-century green glass bottles and flagons in the window were once the staple production of the Swedish and Finnish glassworks, but are now rare examples of what were precious household commodities in a bygone age.

LEFT *A short passage leads from the entrance hall to the* salle, *where the strong symmetry of the Baroque ideal is very much in evidence. This symmetry is presaged in the passage itself, with pairs of garden statues, iron jardinières and benches with* faux *marble tops.*

RIGHT *This bedroom boasts a white glazed tiled stove in Empire style. The walls and bed have been covered in wallpaper and fabric in the same pattern – the design for which was taken from late eighteenth-century woven fabric found at Lövstad Manor in Östergötland.*

The bed shown here is generally called an 'imperial' bed in Sweden – a term in use since the end of the eighteenth century that now covers all pull-out beds that have headboards and footboards and were designed to project into the room from a central position against one wall. The term originated at a time when most Swedish beds were secreted in an alcove and the new type, usually with hangings, was based on royal French beds. The rectangular half-tester was made at the same time as the bed itself, during the 1790s or perhaps the early 1800s. The typical Gustavian dining chair is of similar date.

Drakamöllan

The farmhouse of Drakamöllan, in south-eastern Skåne, stands in the most beautiful and unspoilt countryside of the region. The house's current owners, museum curator Ingemar Tunander and his journalist wife Britt, have made Drakamöllan a source of inspiration for interior decorators and for anyone lovingly renovating their home. The Tunanders have written a number of seminal works on art, crafts and antiques, and at Drakamöllan they have pooled their talents and their impressive knowledge of both building and furniture construction techniques to create an unconventional home which possesses something of the same ability to inspire as the Larssons' home at Sundborn.

PREVIOUS PAGES *The house at Drakamöllan, a traditional, half-timbered southern Swedish cottage thatched with reeds, has regained its historical identity now that it has been painstakingly restored.*

The painted wooden gardener leaning on a spade and puffing his pipe has ancestors in the seventeenth-century figures which once peopled the garden at Sandemar. Here he helps to recapture the seventeenth-century concept of the garden as theatre.

The bedroom is filled with references to the past. The wallpaper is a reproduction of the original that still hangs at Linnaeus's home at Hammarby. It was developed by Ingemar Tunander, a specialist in wallcoverings, whose interest is also apparent in the folding screen covered in paper that is a reprint of an Empire-period pattern.

The black-stained Rococo writing table with its open cabinet dates from the 1700s, and is of the same type as that used in the royal apartments at Gripsholm Castle in the days of Gustav III. The red-brown painted chair with a black wooden seat is a traditional provincial chair from east central Sweden. The green paint and the over-door bookshelf belong to a tradition made fashionable by Carl Larsson at Sundborn. The cast-iron stove was once typical for this part of Sweden and enhances the impression of authenticity.

LEFT *In the largest room a new, wooden floor has been laid in the traditional way with visible nails, and has also been left untreated. Below the height of the window sills, the bookcases are painted light grey, creating an effect similar to the eighteenth-century division of walls by a grey-painted wooden dado. Exquisite antiques mix happily with newly produced items: held aloft by the wings of an eagle, the top of an early nineteenth-century giltwood console table is made of the same Dalarna porphyry as the fruit bowl and butter dish which stand upon it. The medallion on the wall, however, is a modern plaster impression taken from an eighteenth-century original.*

BELOW *The front doors that lead into the entrance hall come from a local village and feature the traditional tongue-and-groove pattern found on doors from Dalarna and Gästrikland.*

The wallpaper frieze of Pompeian griffins and urns is a copy of a late Gustavian design. The walls below are spatter-painted in eighteenth-century tradition with white and black on a light red background to give the impression of granite or light porphyry.

The combination of the reproduction floor and wallpapers with old pieces such as the doors, the provincial late Baroque chest, the veneer-painted clock and the naive painting requires an unerring sense of design if it is to seem as natural as it does here.

Levide

The vicarage at Levide, on the island of Gotland, was built in 1786 during the reign of King Gustav III. It is as large as many of the manor houses that were built on the mainland at that time.

The stone house no longer belongs to the Church, but has been acquired by Evert and Solveig Malmström who have completely renovated it, endeavouring to re-create the original character of the house.

PREVIOUS PAGES *The blue of the window surrounds is peculiar to Gotland. While the window of the timber outhouse (seen in the detail), with its wooden glazing bars, is typically Gustavian, the three large panes of glass, one above the other, in the windows of the main building are probably not original. Panes of glass this size were prohibitively expensive for many years after the vicarage was built.*

The original wall decoration of the salle *has been revealed after the removal of layer upon layer of wallpaper. The walls below the height of the window sills are spatter-painted, and above, are divided into faux panels decorated with stemwork and garlands of flowers against a white background. The loose furnishings, most of them purchased locally on Gotland, exhibit the same faintly provincial qualities as the decoration on the walls.*

RIGHT *Below the red oxide pigment on the walls of what is now the dining room, the imitation panelled dado, painted in shades of grey, is a conventional Gustavian feature. The furniture was all produced on Gotland. Neither the cupboard that dates from 1787, nor the table that is of a similar date, show signs of the influences of Gustavian Classicism: the Baroque lines and Rococo ornamentation reveal how popular provincial taste clung to older styles long after they had ceased to be fashionable on the mainland. The blue-painted chairs do, it is true, have some of the features of late Gustavian design (turned front legs, fluted at seat-rail height), but these were probably produced some years into the nineteenth century.*

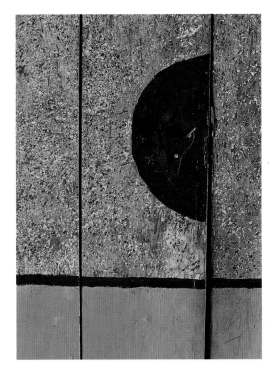

RIGHT *The walls of the small hallway would have been painted first in a light grey shade obtained from lamp-black pigment and then spattered with black and white. This kind of spatter-painting effect was first developed around 1790 to produce a convincing imitation of granite in the pavilion at Haga and at the court theatre at Drottningholm. Below the white boarded ceiling, a pink-painted cornice mimics the contrasting friezes that were so popular during the Empire period.*

ABOVE *The only immediate indication that this is a door and not simply part of the wooden panelling is the black semi-circle, which was painted around the key-hole in the early nineteenth century. This is a device that can also be seen round the escutcheon of an attic door at Odenslunda.*

Odenslunda

ABOVE *When the manor house at Odenslunda was first built, the vertical boards would have been pale yellow, but they have recently been painted white. The original ground plan is revealed by the pilaster-like boxes on the façade: these cover the projecting end timbers of the interior walls.*

LEFT *An 'imperial' bed (see page 172), of the type that can be reduced to half its length when not in use, dominates the bedroom. While the canopy is original, the bed itself is an exact copy of a Gustavian bed. The portraits on either side are of Count Fredrik Gyllenborg, and his wife, Elisabeth Stierncrona, Odenslunda's owners in the mid-eighteenth century. The curtains at the window and the bed hangings are made of cotton, the pattern copied from an eighteenth-century fabric that would have been printed with woodblocks. The long-case clock in the corner has typical Swedish Rococo lines and is decorated with chinoiseries picked out in gilt on the dark brown lacquer.*

RIGHT, ABOVE AND BELOW *What is now a bedroom at Odenslunda leads off the entrance hall, which can be glimpsed through the open door. As much of an eighteenth-century feel as possible has been given to the room: the eighteenth-century columnar stove, installed to replace a worn-out early twentieth-century model, stands on its original wooden base with turned legs in the shape of tiny balusters; the decoration on the whitewashed, papered walls and round the ceilings was copied from a fragment rescued from the now-demolished wing at Sjöholm Manor in Södermanland, and the once-varnished floor has been sanded down to reveal bare floorboards once again. A ruddy-brown painted chair-rail runs along the white painted walls at window-sill height. This moulding, fitted to protect the walls from damage, formed part of the room's original decoration but was moved down to rest on top of the skirting in the early part of the twentieth century. The woodwork round the windows and the doorcases is painted in the same earthy brown shade which was part of the room's original colour scheme. The eighteenth-century bed with camel-back curved posts and a round, crested tester, known as a lit à la polonaise, has been fitted with modern textiles.*

Although the manor house at Odenslunda in Uppland was built in the 1770s during the reign of Gustav III, the *säteri* roof – with its double pitch and small vertical 'waistband' pierced by tiny windows – gives it the air of an older house. At the end of the seventeenth century Samuel Ehrenstedt, one of the courtiers of Queen Ulrika Eleanora the Elder, acquired the medieval farm at Odenslunda and built a new Baroque manor house there comprising a main building and two separate wings – one of which is still standing. Between 1730 and 1771 the estate was owned by the Gyllenborg family, whose portraits hang in the house today. In 1771, when the main building was destroyed by fire, it was immediately re-erected but on a smaller scale, and it is very likely that the new exterior reflected that of the house that had burned down.

LEFT *The kitchen at Odenslunda is housed in a timber annexe attached to the main house that was added in the mid-nineteenth century. The old stove with its brick chimney hood was taken out in the 1940s, but has now been reinstated. The colour scheme – white walls and brown-painted woodwork – is much the same as that in the bedroom seen opposite. The grey-painted drop-leaf table and the chairs were – for practical reasons – copied in the 1970s from the eighteenth-century ones which now stand in another part of the kitchen. The blue-and-white checked cotton roller blinds, too, are copies of eighteenth-century originals.*

The salle at Odenslunda is in the middle of the house, immediately beyond the entrance hall, as was customary in the eighteenth century. The wall timbers were plastered and papered in the middle of the nineteenth century, but when the house was renovated in the 1970s, the walls were covered with distemper and decorated with rectangular panels outlined in pink. The original eighteenth-century painted paper that inspired this scheme was found in another house, and a fragment of paper from there is pasted on the wall adjacent to what appears to be a tiled stove, but which is, in fact, a painted cabinet. This was found, already stripped of its paint, in an antique shop, and then painted blue and white to provide an exact copy of the authentic stove from the 1780s or 1790s which stands in the opposite corner. This was a recognized eighteenth-century trick, devised to achieve symmetry – an all-pervading ideal of the time.

The salle *is furnished in consistently Gustavian fashion with a sizable central drop-leaf table, serving tables along the walls, and painted dining chairs – though two are replicas of the two originals. Lighting is provided by the candles in the glass lantern hanging over the table and on the wall-mounted mirror sconces, which are copies of original eighteenth-century sconces.*

Under previous owners the floors were covered with parquet-patterned linoleum, but now the scrubbed floorboards have been revealed once more, worn and marked by insects as they are. Although the well-worn, hand-knotted Oriental carpet comes from an old Swedish manor house, it is unlikely that carpets like this were used in such modest surroundings as these in the 1700s. Its use here is part of the desire to create a cosy atmosphere – and one which also has the advantages of protecting the wood floor and helping to reduce draughts.

PLACES TO VISIT AND MAP

Sketch map indicating the location of the houses featured in the book

The following museums, castles and manors that are referred to in the text are open to the public. Check their opening hours, especially as many are open only during the summer months.

IN AND CLOSE TO STOCKHOLM
The Chinese Pavilion,
Drottningholm Royal Castle,
Drottningholm
TEL 010 46 8 789 8690

Court Theatre,
Drottningholm
TEL 010 46 8 759 0406

Gustav III's Pavilion,
Haga,
Solna
TEL 010 46 8 789 8500

The Royal Palace,
Gamla Stan
TEL 010 46 8 789 8500

Skansen Open-air Museum,
Djurgårdsslätten 49-51
TEL 010 46 8 442 8000

Svindersvik,
Nacka (Nordiska Museet)
TEL 010 46 8 666 46 00

SOUTH OF STOCKHOLM
Gripsholm Castle,
Mariefred
TEL 010 46 159 101 94

Nynäs,
Tystberga (Södermanlands Museum)
TEL 010 46 155 26 15 05

Sturehov,
Norsborg
TEL 010 468 530 280 11

NORTH OF STOCKHOLM
Almare-Stäket,
Kungsägen
TEL 010 468 583 530 55

Linnaeus's Hammarby,
Hammarby
TEL 010 46 18 32 60 94

Skokloster Castle,
Bålsta
TEL 010 46 18 38 60 77

WEST OF STOCKHOLM,
VÄSTMANLAND
Ängsö,
Västerås
TEL 010 46 171 440 12

Strömsholm Palace,
Kolbäck
TEL 010 46 220 430 35

SOUTH-WEST OF STOCKHOLM,
BOHUSLÄN AND VÄSTERGÖTLAND
Läckö Castle,
Lidköping
TEL 010 46 510 672 00

DALARNA
Carl Larsson's house,
Carl Larsson väg 12,
Sundborn
TEL 010 46 23 600 53

GÄSTRIKLAND
Järbo Hembygdsmuseum,
Sandviken
TEL 010 46 26 27 49 73

HÄLSINGLAND
Karlsgården i Bondarv,
Hembygdsmuseum,
Järvsö,
Ljusdal
TEL 010 46 651 409 47

OSTERGÖTLAND
Medevi Brunn,
Motala
TEL 010 46 141 911 00

GOTLAND
Katthamra,
Katthammarsvik
TEL 010 46 498 520 09

INDEX

Index

OVERLEAF *The great unfurnished* salle *at Hässelbyholm is one of the most beautiful examples of a successful marriage between a seventeenth-century room and eighteenth-century decoration. The house was built in the mid-seventeenth century and the original stucco ceiling was retained when this room was redecorated in the years around 1780. Bronze-coloured ornaments decorate the marbled canvas wall panels, and the doors have been painted to imitate cedar or light mahogany.*

AUTHORS' ACKNOWLEDGMENTS

This book would never have been possible without the generosity and hospitality of all those whose houses are featured in it. We are grateful to all the state-owned museums and institutions who opened their doors to us, and we are especially grateful to all the people who allowed their homes to be photographed, with all the disruption that is inevitably involved. The attraction of our Swedish cultural heritage owes a great deal to the fact that so much still remains within the sphere of privately owned homes, where inherited or acquired furniture and *objets d'art* lend each and every room a sense of authenticity and a character all of its own. However, it is not only the owners of the manor houses and other beautiful homes shown here that we would like to thank. Our gratitude also goes to all those whose homes we have not included because of lack of space.

Lars Sjöberg, Ursula Sjöberg, Ingalill Snitt

PUBLISHERS' ACKNOWLEDGMENTS

The Publishers would like to thank Ian Hinchliffe for his work with the translation, Helen Baz for the index and Hilary Hockman, Sue Gladstone and Auriol Miller for their help in producing this book.

Editorial Director Erica Hunningher
Art Director Caroline Hillier
Production Adela Cory
Production Director Nicky Bowden
Picture Editor Anne Fraser

PHOTOGRAPHIC ACKNOWLEDGMENTS

All photographs by Ingalill Snitt, except for those on the following pages: 51 LEFT (*The Countess's closet at Åkerö c. 1760*), 163 LEFT (*The Flower Window 1894-7* from *Ett Hem*) Nationalmuseum, Stockholm; 161 Nisse Peterson; 95 Fritz von der Schulenburg; 26 BELOW Elizabeth Whiting & Associates/David George

LES TROIS QUESTIONS

d'après un conte de Léon Tolstoï

écrit et illustré par Jon J Muth

ALBUMS
circonflexe

Traduction de l'américain par Catherine Bonhomme

Copyright © 2002 by Jon J Muth
Titre original : The Three Questions
Published by special arrangement
with Scholastic Inc., New York
© 2003, Circonflexe pour l'édition en langue française
ISBN 978-2-87833-589-7
Imprimé en Italie. Dépôt légal : juillet 2011
Loi n° 49-956 du 16 juillet 1949
sur les publications destinées à la jeunesse

Pour Nikolai

Il était une fois un garçon nommé Nikolaï qui se demandait
quelle était la meilleure façon d'agir. « Je veux être quelqu'un de bien,
disait-il à ses amis, mais je ne sais pas toujours comment y parvenir. »
Ses amis comprenaient son désarroi et souhaitaient l'aider.
« Si seulement j'obtenais les réponses aux trois questions qui me hantent,
ajoutait-il, alors je saurais toujours quoi faire. »

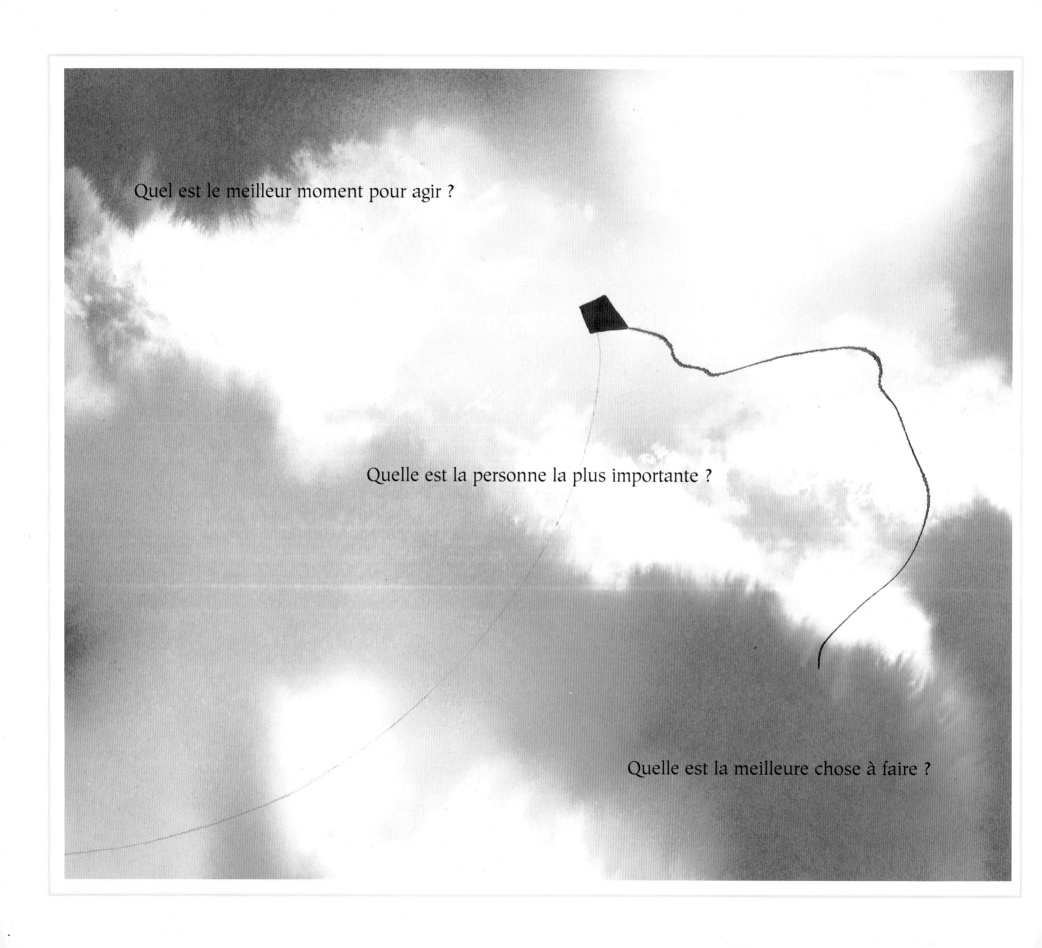

Quel est le meilleur moment pour agir ?

Quelle est la personne la plus importante ?

Quelle est la meilleure chose à faire ?

Les amis de Nikolaï réfléchirent
à sa première question.
Sonya le héron prit la parole :
« Pour savoir quel est le meilleur
moment pour agir, il faut
s'organiser en conséquence. »

Gogol le singe, qui venait
de fourrager dans les feuilles
pour trouver à manger, ajouta :
« Tu sauras à quel moment
il faut agir si tu es attentif
et observateur. »

Et Pouchkine le chien, qui était
sur le point de s'assoupir,
conclut : « Tu ne peux pas
toi seul faire attention à tout.
Tu as besoin d'un gardien
vigilant pour t'aider à décider
quel est le meilleur moment.
À ce propos, Gogol, une noix
de coco risque de te tomber
sur la tête. »

Nikolaï réfléchit un moment.
Puis il posa sa deuxième question.
« Quelle est la personne la plus importante ? »

« Celle qui sait guérir
les malades », proposa Gogol
en frottant sa tête endolorie.

« Celle qui établit les règles »,
grogna Pouchkine.

« Celle qui est le plus près
du paradis », dit Sonya
en décrivant de grands cercles
dans le ciel.

Nikolaï réfléchit à nouveau longuement.
Puis il posa sa troisième question.
« Quelle est la meilleure chose à faire ? »
« Voler », dit Sonya.
« S'amuser tout le temps », s'esclaffa Gogol.
« Se bagarrer », aboya Pouchkine sur-le-champ.

Le garçon demeura silencieux un long moment. Il aimait ses amis.
Il sentait qu'ils faisaient de leur mieux pour l'aider à répondre
à ses trois questions, mais leurs réponses ne le satisfaisaient pas totalement.
Soudain, il lui vint une idée. « Je sais ! Je vais interroger Léon la tortue.
Il vit depuis très longtemps. Il connaît sûrement les réponses à mes questions. »

Nikolaï se mit en route et gravit la montagne où vivait, solitaire et retirée, la vieille tortue.

Lorsqu'il arriva, il trouva Léon en train de bêcher son jardin.
La tortue étant très âgée, bêcher lui demandait de gros efforts.
« Je me pose trois questions et j'ai pensé que tu pourrais m'aider, dit Nikolaï.
Quel est le meilleur moment pour agir ? Quelle est la personne la plus importante ?
Quelle est la meilleure chose à faire ? »

Léon écouta attentivement, mais se contenta de sourire puis recommença à bêcher.
« Tu dois être fatigué, dit Nikolaï au bout d'un moment. Laisse-moi t'aider. »
La tortue lui tendit la bêche et le remercia.
Bêcher est beaucoup plus facile pour un jeune garçon que pour une vieille tortue.
Nikolaï ne s'arrêta qu'après avoir retourné tout le jardin.

Mais juste comme il terminait, le vent
se leva, de gros nuages noirs éclatèrent
et la pluie se mit à tomber.
Or, tandis qu'il se dirigeait vers la maison
de Léon pour s'y abriter, Nikolaï entendit
soudain des pleurs et des appels au secours.

Aussitôt, il dévala le sentier en courant et trouva un panda,
la patte blessée par un arbre que le vent avait déraciné.

Avec précaution, Nikolaï le prit dans ses bras et le transporta
dans la maison de la tortue. Puis, avec une tige de bambou,
il confectionna une attelle pour la patte.

La tempête faisait rage, cognant aux portes et aux fenêtres.
Le panda se réveilla.
« Où suis-je ? s'écria-t-il. Où est mon enfant ? »

Nikolaï se précipita dehors et courut le long du sentier.
La tempête faisait un vacarme assourdissant.
Luttant contre le vent qui hurlait et contre la pluie diluvienne,
il s'enfonça dans la forêt. Et, là, il trouva le petit panda
qui gisait par terre, gelé et tremblant de froid.

Le petit panda était trempé jusqu'aux os et effrayé, mais vivant.
Nikolaï le ramena à la maison. Il le sécha, le réchauffa
et le déposa tendrement dans les bras de sa mère.

Léon sourit en voyant ce qu'avait fait le garçon.

Le lendemain matin, le soleil était de retour,
les oiseaux chantaient, la vie était belle.
Sa patte commençait à guérir, et le panda
remercia Nikolaï de l'avoir sauvé avec son enfant.
C'est juste à cet instant qu'arrivèrent Sonya,
Gogol et Pouchkine. Ils voulaient s'assurer
que tout le monde était sain et sauf.

Nikolaï ressentait une grande paix intérieure.
Il avait des amis merveilleux. Il avait sauvé
le panda et son enfant. Cependant, il était déçu.
Il n'avait toujours pas obtenu de réponses à ses questions.
Il interrogea donc à nouveau Léon.

La vieille tortue l'observa.
« Mais ces réponses, tu les as eues »,
répondit-elle.
« Vraiment ? » demanda Nicolaï.

« Si tu n'étais pas resté hier pour m'aider à bêcher mon jardin,
tu n'aurais pas entendu le panda crier à l'aide à travers la tempête.
C'est pourquoi le moment le plus important a été celui que tu as passé
à retourner mon jardin. La personne la plus importante à cet instant-là,
c'était moi, et la chose la plus importante à faire était de m'aider au jardin.
Par la suite, quand tu as trouvé le panda blessé, le moment le plus important
a été le temps que tu as passé à soigner sa patte et à sauver son enfant.
Les personnes les plus importantes alors étaient le panda et son enfant.
Et la chose la plus importante à faire était de prendre soin d'eux et de les sauver.

« Ainsi rappelle-toi qu'il y a un seul moment important, et que ce moment c'est maintenant.
La personne la plus importante est toujours celle avec laquelle tu es. Et la chose la plus importante
est d'être bon avec la personne qui est à tes côtés. Voilà, mon cher enfant, les réponses à tes questions
sur ce qui est le plus important dans ce monde.

« Et voilà pourquoi nous sommes ici. »

Note de l'auteur

J'ai trouvé mention des « Trois Questions » il y a de nombreuses années dans un livre d'un maître zen vietnamien, Thich Nhat Hanh. Quand je l'ai lue pour la première fois, cette histoire a retenti en moi telle une cloche d'or, comme si je connaissais déjà ce conte par cœur. Certains livres sont ainsi, et cela m'est arrivé très souvent en lisant Léon Tolstoï.

La nouvelle originale ne met pas en scène un garçon et ses amis animaux, mais un tsar à la recherche de réponses aux « trois questions ». L'aventure elle-même est différente. Au lieu de sauver un panda et son enfant, le tsar secourt sans le vouloir un homme qui voulait sa perte. En sauvant son ennemi, il établit une profonde relation avec quelqu'un d'autre. J'encourage vivement les amateurs de récits ingénieux à lire la merveilleuse nouvelle de Tolstoï qui porte ce même titre.

J'ai voulu que cette histoire soit connue des enfants, même si sa forme en est ici quelque peu différente. J'ai conçu cet album comme un hommage à Tolstoï. J'espère qu'il l'aurait fait sourire.

Le nom donné à chaque animal est intentionnel. Pouchkine et Gogol sont ceux d'illustres écrivains russes. Sonya était le prénom de la femme de Tolstoï, Nikolaï celui de son frère, ainsi que de mon propre fils. Quant au personnage du sage incarné par Léon la tortue, il renvoie, bien sûr, à Tolstoï lui-même.

Léon Tolstoï (1828-1910) a été l'un des plus grands romanciers russes et l'un de ses intellectuels et réformateurs les plus influents. Il est très célèbre pour deux de ses œuvres, *Guerre et Paix* (1865-1869) et *Anna Karénine* (1875-1877), et pour avoir été l'un des penseurs les plus exceptionnels du dix-neuvième siècle. Sa nouvelle, « Les Trois Questions », dont cet album est inspiré, a été publiée pour la première fois en 1903.